FACING YOUR GIANTS

STUDY GUIDE

BY MAX LUCADO

NELSON IMPACT

A Division of Thomas Nelson Publishers

Since 1798

www.thomasnelson.com

FACING YOUR GIANTS STUDY GUIDE
Copyright © 2006 Max Lucado

The publishers are grateful to Terry Hadaway for his collaboration, writing skills, and editorial help in developing the content for this study guide.

All rights reserved. No portion of this book may be reproduced, stored in a retrieval system, or transmitted in any form or by any means—electronic, mechanical, photocopy, recording, or any other—except for brief quotations in printed reviews, without the prior written permission of the publisher.

Published by Nelson Impact, a Division of Thomas Nelson, Inc., P.O. Box 141000, Nashville, Tennessee 37214.

Scripture quotations are taken from:

The New King James Version (NKJV), copyright " 1982 by Thomas Nelson, Inc. Used by permission. All rights reserved.

The Holy Bible, New Living Translation (NLT), copyright © 1996. Used by permission of Tyndale House Publishers, Inc., Wheaton, Illinois 60189. All rights reserved.

The Message (MSG) by Eugene H. Peterson, copyright © 1993, 1994, 1995, 1996, 2000, 2001, 2002. Used by permission of NavPress Publishing Group. All rights reserved.

The Holy Bible, New International Version (NIV). Copyright©1973, 1978, 1984 by International Bible Society. Used by permission of Zondervan. All rights reserved.

ISBN-10: 1-4185-1415-2
ISBN-13: 978-1-4185-1415-0

Printed in the United States of America

06 07 08 09 RRD 9 8 7 6 5 4 3 2 1

TABLE OF CONTENTS

Introduction

When was the last time you really faced the "giants" in your life? How long since you ran toward your challenge? We tend to retreat, to duck behind a desk of work or crawl into a nightclub of distraction or a bed of forbidden love. For a moment, a day, or a year, we feel safe, insulated, anesthetized, but then the work runs out, the liquor wears off, or the lover leaves, and we hear Goliath again. Booming. Bombastic.

This is a study of the life of King David—an unlikely hero who was consumed with an awesome God. David's story encompasses both a life of incredible victory and of personal tragedy. In *Facing Your Giants Study Guide,* you will discover what David knew—that God is bigger than any giants you may face in life. Focus on your giants—you stumble. Focus on God—your giants tumble. The God who made a miracle out of David stands ready to make one out of you too.

As you work through this study, you will be challenged by David's devotion and God's provision, and you will learn to face your giants with confidence in God's ability to overcome them.

Each lesson in this study guide features the following sections:

SCRIPTURAL FOCUS: This is the main passage of Scripture for the lesson. To get the most from the lesson, read the passage in its entirety.

LESSON OBJECTIVE: The lesson objective will help you know what to look for in the lesson.

REWIND: In this section, you will take a look at the biblical context for the passage being studied.

RETHINK: Drawing on the foundational principles in the Scripture being studied, you will be challenged to reconsider any thoughts or attitudes you have that might be inconsistent with the Bible.

REFLECT: What would happen if you put these principles to use in your daily life? Would your life change? If so, how?

REACT: Now what? Based on what you learned in this lesson, what will you change about your life?

There also are Small Group Leader Guides in the back of this book that contain additional information and discussion questions to guide you in leading a small group. These guides help make your group sessions easy, effective, and fun.

Giants. We must face them. Yet, we need not face them alone. Learn to focus first, and most, on God.

Let's begin.

1

FACING YOUR GIANTS

⚜

Scriptural Focus: 1 Samuel 17:1–11

LESSON OBJECTIVE: To discover how problems affect our lives and commit to trusting God to overcome them

> The Philistines stood on a mountain on one side, and Israel stood on a mountain on the other side, with a valley between them. (1 Samuel 17:3 NKJV)

REWIND: There was nothing about the situation that would have made for a good story line. David, the boyish shepherd was offering to go toe-to-toe with the behemoth, Goliath. It resembled one of those preseason baseball games that pit college players against major leaguers. The outcome usually is predictable; the only unknown is how bad it will be.

David's preparation involves stopping by the creek to collect a few stones—a good idea if you are protecting sheep from predators; a bad idea if you are fighting a giant! But the size of the stones had nothing to do with David's success against Goliath. David's real strength came from his relationship with God. God knew that. David knew that. Goliath and the Philistines didn't have confidence in God, they taunted him. Therein lies the real story. The battle isn't a battle between a boy and a giant, but God-focus versus self-focus. Goliath thought he couldn't be beat. And he was right. . . . at least from the world's perspective.

RETHINK: Your Goliath comes in different shapes and sizes. To the casual observer, it looks as if you can't win. Your giant taunts you publicly and you are left to gather rocks. Though the situation looks hopeless, you know better. The giant is too big and you are too weak. But you have a secret weapon—a power not understood by casual observers.

In what areas of life are you most taunted by "giants"?

☐ unemployment
☐ abandonment
☐ sexual abuse
☐ depression
☐ finances
☐ morality
☐ education
☐ other: _____

Just the mention of your giant has an emotional effect on you. Your giant elicits anxiety, shame, confusion, or anger. He might not stand in the Valley of Elah, but he calls to you at the most inopportune times. In David's day, the focus always had been on the giant; but David's strategy was different.

Think about the giants that concern you most.

How does the average day begin for you?

I think about the giants <———————————————> I think about God

This wasn't the first time the Israelites had been dogged by the Philistines. History taught the Israelites that the Philistines would win, so going into battle against them was futile. Maybe you suffer with the same problem—you aren't the first person in your family to face this enemy and history doesn't give you much hope for winning the battle.

David knew that Israel would keep getting what it was getting if it kept doing what it was doing. The nation was paralyzed because it focused on the enemy. David was empowered because he refused to tip his cap to the enemy; his focus was on God.

You've been on your own exodus and experienced God's power first hand. In the space below, list some personal examples of God's miraculous work in your life.

Based on your past experience with God, which of the statements is true?

☐ I have no reason to trust God.
☐ I have plenty of reasons to trust God.

REFLECT: Read 1 Samuel 17:1–11. Saul and the Israelites looked as if they were ready to battle the Philistines (v. 2), but they were afraid (v. 11).

Have you ever been in a similar situation when facing one of your giants? If so, how did your fear affect your determination?

There was only one viable option: God's people had to rely on God to win the battle. The simple faith of a shepherd boy teaches a valuable spiritual lesson: Focus on giants—you stumble. Focus on God—your giants tumble.

Lift your eyes, giant slayer. The God who made a miracle out of David stands ready to make one out of you.

REACT: You have a choice: battle your giants in your own power, run from your giants, allow your giants to paralyze you, or turn your giants over to God and let him overcome them. It's your choice . . . what's it going to be?

"Then David put his hand in his bag and took out a stone; and he slung it and struck the Philistine in his forehead, so that the stone sank into his forehead, and he fell on his face to the earth" (1 Samuel 17:49 NKJV).

Do you remember those stones David picked up from the creek bank? They usually weren't effective in killing giants. But God took an ordinary boy with ordinary tools and accomplished an extraordinary feat. What about you? What giant is ridiculing you from the mountain?

What is preventing God from slaying the giants in your life?

Based on what God taught me in this lesson, I will:

2

SILENT PHONES

⚜

Scriptural Focus: 1 Samuel 16:1–13

LESSON OBJECTIVE: To discover the qualities that led to David's becoming king and commit to developing those qualities in our lives

> Then Samuel took the horn of oil and anointed him in the midst of his brothers; and the Spirit of the LORD came upon David from that day forward. So Samuel arose and went to Ramah. (1 Samuel 16:13 NKJV)

REWIND: In 1000 B.C. being a king was a big deal. Most of the nations surrounding Israel had one, and Israel needed one—a strong one! Though Saul was referred to as king, he had never really been appointed as king. He was the *nagid* or military leader; Israel didn't really have a *melek*, or king.

The *nagid* was selected for military purposes; to be a *melek* took character. Saul was acting like the king but he lacked kingly character. So God impeached him and instructed Samuel to go visit Jesse in Bethlehem—one of his eight sons had kingly character.

Samuel approaches Jesse and asks to see his sons. By the world's standards, the first seven brothers were king material. But God told Samuel, "No." Seven sons down and no king. Samuel must have been wondering what was up. So, Jesse called for his youngest son, David. Up to this point, Jesse hadn't seen the need to summon David from his shepherding tasks. After all, he was just a shepherd.

Describe a time when God did something that surprised you.

Isn't it funny how God often picks the least likely person to accomplish his tasks? God turned down charisma, good looks, and physical stature, and he selected young David to lead Israel. Least likely people often make a huge impact for God!

RETHINK: When God looks at you he sees beyond the things the world sees. From the list below, check the characteristics you believe are important to God.

☐ appearance	☐ honesty	☐ integrity
☐ faithfulness	☐ possessions	☐ education
☐ wealth	☐ character	☐ personality
☐ intelligence	☐ religion	☐ God-fearing
☐ wardrobe	☐ popularity	☐ humility

Jesse's other sons weren't necessarily bad; they just weren't what God was looking for in a king. Had Samuel selected the king without listening for God's confirmation, he would have selected the wrong son. But Samuel got the confirmation he sought when the least likely of the brothers appeared.

Why does God often use the most unlikely person to accomplish great things for him?

What was it that made David God's choice? When you spend a lot of time with sheep, you probably talk to God . . . a lot! David's shepherding experience taught him that he had to depend on God; he had no other choice.

REFLECT: Maybe you've learned a lot about God through some trying times in your own life.

Describe one of those times and list one or two things you learned about God through that experience.

Read 1 Samuel 16:1–13. The situation in Israel was unusual. Saul was still alive, but ineffective. Israel was threatened from the outside by the Philistines and from the inside by spiritual decay. The problem required a unique solution. Pressures from the outside and decay from the inside required a leader who was tuned in to God.

When things get tough in your life, are you more likely to . . .

- ☐ take care of things yourself?
- ☐ turn everything over to God?

How do you think the older brothers felt when they were passed over in favor of their younger brother?

What qualities did David have that made him a good choice for king?

To what degree do you have the qualities listed on the previous page?

- ☐ David and I are basically twins!
- ☐ David has some things going for him that I don't have, but we're close.
- ☐ David is way ahead of me!
- ☐ That's not me!

David's character qualified him to be used by God. Based on your character, how qualified to be used by God are you?

- ☐ I'm ready to go!
- ☐ I have a little work to do.
- ☐ Uh oh!

In what areas of life do you most need to develop godly character? (check all that apply)

- ☐ home
- ☐ work
- ☐ school
- ☐ recreation/leisure
- ☐ relationships
- ☐ thought life

REACT: You control those things to which you fix your heart. Anything—other than God—to which you focus your attention can easily become a giant in your life. Had David let his mind wander away from God, he might have been unprepared for the role for which God selected him. He chose instead to be faithful to God while being a shepherd, and in the process he became the king.

"So he sent and brought him in. How he was ruddy, with bright eyes, and good-looking. And the LORD said, "Arise, anoint him; for this is the one!" (1 Samuel 16:12 NKJV).

For what role might God be preparing you? How might your attention get diverted so that you spend your time focusing on your giants rather than God's plan?

Based on what God taught me in this lesson, I will:

3

RAGING SAULS

Scriptural Focus: 1 Samuel 18:1–16

LESSON OBJECTIVE: To discover how God is faithful to those who trust and obey him and commit to a lifestyle of obedience to God

> Now Saul was afraid of David, because the LORD was with him, but had departed from Saul. (1 Samuel 18:12 NKJV)

REWIND: David did what no one before him had even attempted—he went one-on-one with Goliath, the Philistine. Relying on God rather than his own strength, David defeated and killed the giant. David's victory gave the Israelites total control over the Philistines. That's what Goliath promised if he was defeated and killed (1 Samuel 17:9). When the Philistines realized Goliath was dead, they started running. For years they had antagonized the Israelites and now it was payback time!

The Israelites chased the Philistines for a while and then returned to the Philistine camp and plundered it like pirates invading a galleon. David collected his own souvenirs—Goliath's head and armor (17:54). He kept the armor in his tent and took Goliath's head to Jerusalem.

At this point Saul begins to concern himself with David and the consequences of his very popular defeat of the Philistines. Jealousy began to bubble deep inside Saul.

Put yourself in David's position. How have your accomplishments been received by others?

Put yourself in Saul's position. How have you been jealous of the accomplishments of others?

The nemesis of the Israelites had been defeated, yet Saul was more concerned about how people would compare him to David. Remember when God removed his spirit from Saul? Well, from that point on, Saul and David were not on the same spiritual team. And not being on the same spiritual team opens up all kinds of interpersonal problems!

RETHINK: The "raging Sauls" in your life come from a variety of sources. In the list below, mark all of the "raging Sauls" in your life.

- ☐ spouse
- ☐ extended family
- ☐ coworker
- ☐ boss
- ☐ friend

- ☐ neighbor
- ☐ someone at church
- ☐ former employer
- ☐ ex-spouse
- ☐ other: _____

Describe one of the dangers posed by one of the sources you identified.

Saul tried to kill David six different times and failed each time. David became more puzzled with each attempt. All he had done was kill Goliath and eliminate the Philistine threat to Israel. Wasn't that what Saul wanted?

In spite of the good things David did, Saul continued to stalk him.

Why do you think Saul sought to kill David?

Saul allowed jealousy to take over. Sure he wanted the Philistines gone, but he wanted credit for it. He wanted the people to applaud him. So, when David was cheered for his conquest, Saul didn't participate.

REFLECT: You might be a David—are you being pursued by someone or something from your past? The good news is that you're not the first person to face such a situation. The better news is that God has a lot of experience sustaining his people during their difficult times. God sent David a Jonathan.

You might get a Jonathan or a Mary or a total stranger or something else. The fact is that God does not leave his people to deal with life's struggles alone.

Describe a time when God sent someone or something to encourage you through a difficult situation.

Read 1 Samuel 18:1–16. The relationship between David and Jonathan was unusual. David's nemesis, Saul, was Jonathan's father. Jonathan chose allegiance to David over allegiance to his family. He chose God-focus over self-focus.

David assumed a position in the court of a lunatic. Let's be honest, some people can relate to David in their jobs! David had some choices:

1. Go out into public and bad-mouth his "boss" and his organization while accepting the benefits of working for them.

2. Go out in public and do as little as necessary in order to collect his paycheck. He could take longer than allowed lunch breaks, manipulate the rules, and spend company time on personal projects.
3. Go out and faithfully fulfill his responsibilities as if he was working for God, not the lunatic.

Read 1 Samuel 18:5.

Which choice did David make? (circle one)

1   2   3

David did what was right, and God blessed and protected him. The same God-focus that allowed him to defeat Goliath sustained him through this interpersonal and seemingly unfair situation. It is evident that Jonathan was a huge encouragement to David. We all need a Jonathan, don't we?

What God-focused person has God brought into your life to help keep you focused on him?

In what ways does the person listed above keep you God-focused?

REACT: Focusing on the "raging Sauls" in your life might prevent you from seeing God's desire for you. Only as David focused on God was he able to survive Saul's repeated attacks. Your Sauls might keep attacking, but your focus on God will strengthen you. There is nothing coming your way that God isn't able to overcome . . . if you will focus on him!

Think back to the "raging Sauls" you marked in the activity earlier in this lesson.

Describe how you can deliberately focus more on God and less on the threats.

Memorize Matthew 28:20 to help you combat your times of personal doubt.

Wander freely and daily through the gallery of God's goodness. Catalogue his kindnesses. Everything from sunsets to salvation—look at what you have. Your Saul took much, but Christ gave you more! Let Jesus be the friend you need. Talk to him. Spare no detail. Disclose your fear and describe your dread.

Will your Saul disappear? Who knows? And, in a sense, does it matter? You just found a friend for life. What could be better than that?

Based on what God taught me in this lesson, I will:

4

DESPERATE DAYS

Scriptural Focus: 1 Samuel 21:1–9

LESSON OBJECTIVE: To realize how God sustains us even when we are desperate and to commit to trusting God through the good times and the bad

> So the priest gave him holy bread; for there was no bread there but the showbread which had been taken from before the LORD, in order to put hot bread in its place on the day when it was taken away. (1 Samuel 21:6 NKJV)

REWIND: David was on the run! Saul's jealousy blossomed into a murder plot that resulted in Jonathan—Saul's son—choosing David over Saul. As David ran, he came to the city of Nob, the city just outside Jerusalem in which a large number of priests lived. They had moved there to escape the destruction of the sanctuary at Shiloh in 1000 B.C. Needless to say, David was a desperate man who was running for his life. The enemy seemed large and his chances of surviving Saul's pursuit seemed slim.

Though David was a fugitive, few people knew it. Unlike today, news back then traveled slowly. Ahimelech met David as he entered the city and wondered out loud why David was traveling alone. Remember . . . desperate people do desperate things! David lied. It wasn't a little white lie; it was a full-blown untruth! For those of us who thought David was more than human, we now know differently!

Maybe you've been in a situation like David. The walls were closing in, the pressure was building, you were running out of options, and you compromised your values. Maybe you lied, stole something, or engaged in an inappropriate relationship. What you did reveals a character flaw. We all have them, but that doesn't give us a license to do what we want.

When the pressure is on, in what ways are you tempted to compromise your values and/or convictions?

Put yourself in David's position. How have you been pressured into doing the wrong thing?

David rationalized his actions so that he could accomplish his objectives. Certainly no one today does that—or do they?

RETHINK: We can agree that most of us do things we know we shouldn't do. As a matter of fact, most of us can find someone or something on which to blame our bad choices.

When you do something you know you shouldn't do, which of the following are you likely to blame? (check all that apply)

☐ government   ☐ other people   ☐ kids
☐ boss   ☐ financial pressure   ☐ social pressure
☐ other: _____

Why do you blame these people and/or situations?

REFLECT: Read 1 Samuel 21:1–9. In spite of David's lie, God showed mercy and compassion. The priest decided that giving David the holy bread was the best thing to do—even though it violated the religious law. Describe a time when God was merciful and generous to you even though your actions betrayed your relationship with him.

Review the passage and identify the three lies David told.

List below each lie and its corresponding truth.

Lie	Truth
1. (v. 2)	
2. (v. 5)	
3. (v. 8)	

David first said that he was on the king's business, when in fact he was running from the king. Secondly, David claimed he and his men were ceremoniously clean, yet Scripture shows nothing to back up his claim. The last thing on David's mind was keeping the religious laws! Finally, David claimed his mission was in such haste that he was unable to gather his weapons. The fact was that David had no weapons to gather!

REACT: Even though David lied, God provided bread for him. God has a way of meeting our needs even when we might believe we don't deserve to have our needs met. Describe a time when you didn't deserve God's provision, but he provided for you anyway.

Peter cowers in the corner and covers his ears, but he can't silence the sound of his empty promise. "I'd die for you," he vowed (Luke 22:33 MSG). But his courage melted in the midnight fire and fear. And now he and the other runaways wonder what place God has for them. Jesus answers the question by walking through the door.

He brings bread for their souls. "Peace be with you" (John 20:19 NIV). He brings a sword for struggle. "Receive the Holy Spirit" (v. 22).

Bread and swords. He gives both to the desperate . . . still.

Are you still amazed at God's provision for you? Do you find yourself shaking your head wondering what you did to deserve such blessings? You don't deserve them; God gives them to the undeserving, the desperate, people like me and you!

Based on what God taught me in this lesson, I will:

5

DRY SEASONS

❦

Scriptural Focus: 1 Samuel 21:10–22:5

LESSON OBJECTIVE: To discover God's presence in the midst of personal struggles and commit to look for God's encouragement in the people he brings into our lives

> David therefore departed from there and escaped to the cave of Adullam. So when his brothers and all his father's house heard it, they went down there to him. And everyone who was in distress, everyone who was in debt, and everyone who was discontented gathered to him. So he became captain over them. And there were about four hundred men with him. (1 Samuel 22:1–2 NKJV)

REWIND: Saul was still on David's trail, so David couldn't stay in one place very long. Saul made helping David a crime punishable by death, so David lost his support structure. He was alone and on the run. After leaving Nob, David headed to Gath—the Philistine city that was home to Goliath and his family. David's notoriety had spread, so it seemed everyone knew who he was.

When David arrived in Gath, he feared the repercussions of having defeated the Philistines and killing Goliath. David, therefore, decided to pretend to be insane. Achish, the king of Gath, wanted nothing to do with David, so David fled to the cave of Adullam. Adullam was about ten miles southeast of Gath and approximately sixteen miles southwest of Jerusalem.

David attracted a following of people who were much like him—distressed for one reason or another. At the cave of Adullam, they banded together and David was recognized as being in charge.

21

To whom or to what do you turn when you are distressed?

So here's our hero . . . hiding in a cave with a band of social misfits who were running for their lives and looking for a leader.

RETHINK: We all have dry seasons. You know what it's like. It seems that everything is more difficult. Easy things become hard. Hard things become harder. And some things just become downright impossible. Life is a chore.

When you find yourself in a dry season, what are you most likely to do?

- ☐ Have a pity-party and feel sorry for myself
- ☐ Become an "anxiety evangelist" and try to convince others to join me in my misery
- ☐ Ignore the situation and pretend it doesn't exist
- ☐ Spend extra time in Bible study and prayer seeking God's direction for my life
- ☐ other: _____

What do you hope to be the outcome of your selected action?

What do you think God might want to accomplish through the dry seasons in your life?

REFLECT: Read 1 Samuel 21:10–22:5. One of the more amazing elements of this story is the attraction of the people to David.

Why do you think the people were so attracted to him?

What kinds of people are attracted to you and why do you think they are attracted?

Once again, God sent someone with a message to David. The prophet Gad told him to go to Judah, so David did as he was told.

Who has God sent to help you determine his will for your life?

How do you know who to listen to?

- ☐ I like the person a lot.
- ☐ He or she tells me what I want to hear.
- ☐ He or she tells me to do what I already had decided to do.
- ☐ He or she helps me interpret Scripture so that it is easier to obey.
- ☐ He or she speaks the truth and never knowingly contradicts Scripture.

God might be equipping you to be an advisor to someone else. What are some things you are doing to be better prepared to be used by God in the lives of others?

- ☐ Nothing. I don't have time for other people.
- ☐ I go to church when I can.
- ☐ I spend time daily with God and study his Word so that I will know him better.

REACT: David ran, but God still used him.

Describe a time when God has used you in spite of your running from him.

Are you in the wilderness? Crawl into God like a fugitive would a cave. Find refuge in God's presence.

Find comfort in his people. Cast your hat in a congregation of folks who are one gift of grace removed from tragedy, addiction, and disaster. Seek community in the church of Adullam.

Seek refuge in God's presence. Find comfort in God's people. These are your keys for wilderness survival. Do this and, who knows, in the midst of this desert you may write your sweetest psalms.

Take a few moments and write a prayer of praise expressing to God your thoughts about one of your wilderness experiences. Don't be afraid to be honest; he already knows what you're thinking anyway!

Based on what God taught me in this lesson, I will:

6

GRIEF GIVERS

✿

Scriptural Focus: 1 Samuel 24:1–15

LESSON OBJECTIVE: To discover God's grace and commit to extending that grace to everyone we encounter

> So David restrained his servants with these words, and did not allow them to rise against Saul. And Saul got up from the cave and went on his way. David also arose afterward, went out of the cave, and called out to Saul, saying, 'My lord the king!' And when Saul looked behind him, David stooped with his face to the earth, and bowed down. (1 Samuel 24:7–8 NKJV)

REWIND: Saul's anger against David extended to those David encountered while he ran. While Saul killed the priests at Nob, David fled to Keilah, about eighteen miles southwest of Jerusalem. Keilah was under attack from the Philistines, so God instructed David to defend the city. But David's men weren't so keen on the idea of interrupting their flight from Saul in order to fight a Philistine army. David went to God a second time asking, "Uh, God, are you sure about this fighting the Philistines thing?" God was sure; it was David and his men who were struggling with the situation.

Describe a time when you questioned God about something he told you to do.

So David and his men defended the city of Keilah and defeated the Philistines. Keilah was a walled city, so escape from it was limited. When Saul heard David was there, he directed his men to besiege the city and trap David within the walls. David, however, had an advantage. In his conversations with God, he was told that Saul was coming and that the men of Keilah would hand David over to Saul.

When you run from danger, where do you go?

- ☐ a relationship with another person
- ☐ a self-destructive habit
- ☐ a spending spree
- ☐ I turn inward and shut out everyone else.
- ☐ I turn to God first and always.

Do you see the change in David? It seems he has experienced a bit of a revival. Now he is back to speaking to God about his decisions rather than trusting his own instincts. You're just like David . . . but which David best represents your actions?

RETHINK: Grief often comes in the form of a person. That's what David discovered. David's major concern came from Saul—jealous, angry, vindictive Saul. David has every reason to despise Saul and even had opportunities to eliminate Saul's threat. Yet David acted with mercy toward the one who sought to harm him.

What is your attitude toward those who seek to harm you?

- ☐ Get them before they get a chance to get me
- ☐ Run fast
- ☐ Show mercy to them and let God judge
- ☐ other: _____

Describe a situation in which someone has sought to harm you. How did you respond? Was your response the right one?

REFLECT: Read 1 Samuel 24:1–15. In your opinion, what is the most amazing element of this story?

Think back for a moment. David knew that he would be the next king of Israel so eliminating Saul would accelerate his rise to the throne. If David had been self-centered, he would have killed Saul and taken his place as king. David, however, understood the value of God's timing and didn't try to make God's will conform to his personal plans. Don't you wish we could get that idea right?

Describe a time when you failed to wait for God's timing regarding an action or decision. What was the ultimate outcome of the situation?

Why is it so difficult to wait for God?

REACT: Saul was David's number one nemesis, yet David passed on his chance to eliminate the threat. What should be your attitude toward those who pose threats to you?

Only God assesses accurate judgments. We impose punishments too slight or severe. God dispenses perfect justice. Vengeance is his job. Leave your enemies in God's hands.

You're not endorsing their misbehavior when you do. You can hate what someone did without letting hatred consume you. Forgiveness is not excusing.

To forgive is to move on, not think about the offense anymore. You don't excuse him, endorse her, or embrace them. You just route thoughts about them through heaven. You see your enemy as God's child and revenge as God's job.

By the way, how can we grace recipients do anything less? Dare we ask God for grace when we refuse to give it? This is a huge issue in Scripture. Jesus was tough on sinners who refused to forgive other sinners. Remember his story about the servant, freshly forgiven a debt of millions, who refused to forgive a debt of pennies? He stirred the wrath of God, "You evil servant! I forgave you that tremendous debt . . . Shouldn't you have mercy . . . just as I had mercy on you?" (Matthew 18:32–33 NLT).

In the final sum, we give grace because we've been given grace. We survive because we imitate the Survivor Tree. We reach our roots beyond the bomb zone. We tap into moisture beyond the explosion. We dig deeper and deeper, until we draw moisture from the mercy of God.

We, like Saul, have been given grace.

We, like David, can freely give it.

Based on what God taught me in this lesson, I will:

7

BARBARIC BEHAVIOR

Scriptural Focus: 1 Samuel 25:14–38

LESSON OBJECTIVE: To discover how one's commitment to God can overcome that person's self-centeredness

Please forgive the trespass of your maidservant. For the LORD will certainly make for my lord an enduring house, because my lord fights the battles of the LORD, and evil is not found in you throughout your days. (1 Samuel 25:28 NKJV)

REWIND: With Saul appeased for the moment, David turned his attention to Nabal, a ruthless, self-centered barbarian with little concern for anyone but himself. Nabal lived in Maon not far from the stronghold in which David and his men sought refuge. When David heard that Nabal was preparing a huge feast, he sent ten messengers to ask for food. Nabal scoffed at the idea and even acted as if he didn't know who David was. The news of Nabal's reaction so angered David that he gathered four hundred of his men and set off to kill Nabal and his family.

Have you ever acted selfishly? In what areas are you most likely to be selfish?

- ☐ my time
- ☐ my money
- ☐ my talents or skills
- ☐ my home
- ☐ other: _____

Nabal's selfishness made it tough for anyone—including his wife—to enjoy being around him. Is your selfishness affecting the way people respond to you?

RETHINK: Nabal's self-centeredness was a giant in his life. He saw nothing apart from his own desires. He lived to please himself and cared little for anyone else. The people who surrounded him were there out of fear, not devotion.

Sometimes it is easier to gain power by exercising our personal wills. Even though we know we are alienating our friends and families, we still respond to people in ways that degrade them and make them feel stupid. It often is excused by saying, "Well, that's just the way I am."

Maybe you don't see yourself as notorious as Nabal, but what are some things you are prone to do that might make others not want to be around you?

REFLECT: Read 1 Samuel 25:14–38. Abigail to the rescue! One of Nabal's servants recounted to Abigail how gracious David and his men had been to them. She was appalled at Nabal's rejection of David's request for food. When Abigail saw what was about to happen, she came up with a plan to intervene so that David's men would be fed and Nabal's family would be saved.

Describe a time when you have experienced kindness from an unlikely person.

Abigail took responsibility for Nabal's actions. When it comes to difficult situations, are you more likely to blame someone else or take personal responsibility even if someone else was at fault?

Based on Abigail's model, what should you do?

REACT: Our world is full of Nabals. We work with them, live beside them, marry them, and even go to church with them. There's no escaping the Nabals in our lives. Yet we can put our Nabals in proper perspective and maintain our faithfulness to God in spite of their selfishness.

In the space below, list three things you can do to keep your Nabals in proper perspective.

1.

2.

3.

Christ lived the life we could not live, took the punishment we could not take, to offer the hope we cannot resist. His sacrifice begs us to ask this question. If he so loved us, can we not love each other? Having been forgiven, can we not forgive? Having feasted at the table of grace, can we not share a few crumbs? "My dear, dear friends, if God loved us like this, we certainly ought to love each other" (1 John 4:11 MSG).

Do you find your Nabal-world hard to stomach? Then do what David did: stop staring at Nabal. Shift your gaze to Christ. Look more at the Mediator and less at the troublemakers. "Don't let evil get the best of you; get the best of evil by doing good" (Romans 12:21 MSG). One prisoner can change a camp. One Abigail can save a family. Be the beauty amidst your beasts and see what happens.

Based on what God taught me in this lesson, I will:

8

SLUMP GUNS

⚜

Scriptural Focus: 1 Samuel 27:1–4; 30:1–6

LESSON OBJECTIVE: To learn the warning signs of spiritual weariness and to commit to focusing on your relationship to God

> Now David was greatly distressed, for the people spoke of stoning him, because the soul of all the people was grieved, every man for his sons and daughters. But David strengthened himself in the LORD his God. (1 Samuel 30:6 NKJV)

REWIND: Following the death of Nabal, David took Abigail (Nabal's widow) and Ahinoam as wives. With his agreement with Saul fresh on his mind, David dismissed Saul as a source of danger. But he was wrong. The Ziphites told Saul where David was hiding, so Saul gathered three thousand men and headed for the Wilderness of Ziph. David sent out spies to assess the threat and determined that Saul had indeed broken his promise and was back on David's trail. David acted first. He went to Saul's camp but once again refused to kill Saul. Instead, he took Saul's spear and his jug of water. Once a safe distance away, David called back to Saul's camp making Saul and his men aware that he could have killed Saul but chose to show mercy. Once again Saul repented and promised safety for David in return for the mercy David showed him. Saul departed the area and David went about his business.

Dealing with Saul had been stressful. David apparently was exhausted and sought to escape Saul once and for all. Desperate people do desperate things. He decided to seek refuge in Philistia, the home of Israel's chief rivals. David believed Saul would finally give up looking for him.

What are those things that threaten to get the best of you?

- ☐ alcohol or drugs
- ☐ possessions
- ☐ obsession with appearance
- ☐ immoral activity
- ☐ religion (as opposed to a relationship with God)
- ☐ work
- ☐ other: _____

The things you marked are your Sauls. They taunt you and threaten you to the point of wanting to do anything to escape them.

RETHINK: David pledged his allegiance to Achish and was given the town of Ziklag. He raided the neighboring Philistine towns but reported to Achish that he had raided cities in Judah. Achish was certain that all of the Israelites would hate David and that he would have no choice but to remain enslaved to Achish and the Philistines.

Maybe you don't see yourself as aligned with the enemy, but you might see situations in your life where you are prone to compromise your values. For all practical purposes, compromising your values or principles is the same as siding with the enemy.

Describe one situation in which you were challenged to compromise your principles but you refused.

REFLECT: Read 1 Samuel 27:1–4 and 30:1–6.

You are aware of a time when you were challenged to compromise your values but decided not to do so. But what about that time when you did compromise? How did you feel after you sought refuge with the enemy?

Weary from his endless running, David lost hope. Read 1 Samuel 27:1 again.

In the space below rewrite that verse in your own words substituting the thing to which you run for Saul's name.

For example, "Someday my desire for possessions is going to get the best of me, so I might as well escape the threat by indulging in immoral behavior." The line of reasoning doesn't make sense, but desperate people seldom do!

REACT: David has given us reason to wonder what he might do when he returns to Ziklag and discovers that the Amalekites had visited. Not only had they invaded the town, but they burned it and took captive all of the families of David's men. Snuggling up with the enemy makes you vulnerable to other threats. Your family, your home, your present, and your future can't escape the danger. In the end, even those closest to you might change their attitudes toward you. Seeking refuge with the enemy isn't such a good idea after all!

David did. Right there in the smoldering ruins of Ziklag he found strength. After sixteen months in Gath, after the Philistine rejection, the Amalekite attack, and the insurrection by his men, he remembered what to do. "David found strength in the LORD his God" (1 Samuel 30:6 NIV).

It's good to have you back, David. We missed you while you were away.

Based on what God taught me in this lesson, I will:

9

PLOPPING POINTS

Scriptural Focus: 1 Samuel 30:7–25

LESSON OBJECTIVE: To develop an awareness of God's providence and to commit to honoring others in accordance with God's attitude toward us

> But David said, "My brethren, you shall not do so with what the LORD has given us . . . For who will heed you in this matter? But as his part is who goes down to the battle, so shall his part be who stays by the supplies; they shall share alike." (1 Samuel 30:23a, 24 NKJV)

REWIND: Ziklag was in ruins, the women and children were in captivity, the army was in disarray, and David was seeking God's guidance. He went to Abiathar, the priest. Abiathar delivers the ephod to David. This portion of the story represents a spiritual shift in David's life. When he teamed up with the Philistines, he didn't seek God's advice. As a result, things didn't turn out so well. Now he turns to God and is told to pursue the Amalekites.

When are you most likely to seek God's advice on a matter?

☐ when things are going well
☐ when life is chaotic
☐ never
☐ always . . . even when ordering at a fast food restaurant

RETHINK: David and his six hundred men began to chase the Amalekites but weren't sure where they had gone. Their first stop was at the Brook Besor, about fifteen miles south of Ziklag. There two hundred of David's men rested while the remaining four hundred pursued the Amalekites. David's pursuit of the Amalekites can represent our spiritual lives. Sometimes we join the battle and at other times we sit by the brook and let others do the work.

Where are you right now? Are you in the battle or sitting by the brook? Explain your response.

REFLECT: Read 1 Samuel 30:7–25. With the help of an Egyptian left behind by the Amalekites, David and his men located and attacked the Amalekites and recovered their families and property. Only four hundred Amalekites escaped David's ambush. With their families and herds in tow, David and his men returned to the Brook Besor where the two hundred resting soldiers remained.

If you had been a part of the army that defeated the Amalekites, what might have been your reaction to the resting soldiers?

Describe a time when you have rested and let someone else take care of your spiritual responsibility.

It's easy to hand off our jobs. We entrust our children to others for spiritual education. We leave evangelism to the "professionals" hired by the church. We hope someone will talk to our neighbors about getting involved in church. We wonder why there are no teachers for the Bible study classes. While needs go unmet, we sit at the Brook Besor . . . resting.

REACT: Some people hang out at the Brook Besor. If you are listed among them, here is what you need to know: it's okay to rest. Jesus is your David. He fights when you cannot. He goes where you cannot. He's not angry if you sit. Did he not invite, "Come off by yourselves; let's take a break and get a little rest" (Mark 6:31 MSG)?

Describe a time when you have been the recipient of something undeserved.

Brook Besor blesses rest. Brook Besor also cautions against arrogance. David knew the victory was a gift. Let's remember the same. Salvation comes like the Egyptian in the desert, a delightful surprise on the path. Unearned. Undeserved. Who are the strong to criticize the tired?

Are you weary? Catch your breath. We need your strength. Are you strong? Reserve passing judgment on the tired. Odds are you'll need to plop down yourself. And when you do, Brook Besor is a good story to know.

Based on what God taught me in this lesson, I will:

10

UNSPEAKABLE GRIEF

❧

Scriptural Focus: 2 Samuel 1:4–12

LESSON OBJECTIVE: To discover how grief affects us and to commit to trusting God in times of grief

> Therefore David took hold of his own clothes and tore them, and so did all the men who were with him. (2 Samuel 1:11 NKJV)

REWIND: During the battle with the Philistines, Jonathan and two of his brothers were killed. Saul was seriously injured and it was just a matter of time before the Philistines finished him off. He instructed his armor bearer to kill him with a sword, but the armor bearer refused. Saul, therefore, fell on his own sword and killed himself. The remaining men of Israel fled and the Philistines took over the area.

Think back to David's encounters with Saul. How would you describe his attitude toward the king?

David also had a close relationship with Jonathan. News of the deaths of Saul and Jonathan hit David hard. He was grieved.

What personal situation has caused you great grief?

RETHINK: David could have viewed the situation selfishly. After all, he was about to become king of Israel. Yet he was heart-broken because of the loss of God's leader for his nation and his close friend. Grief has a way of minimizing personal differences. It's too bad that many people choose to let their differences persist until death.

Is there someone with whom you need to restore a personal relationship? If so, list that person and what you will do to restore the relationship.

REFLECT: Read 2 Samuel 1:4–12. An Amalekite who witnessed the deaths of Saul and Jonathan reported the situation to David. He even delivered to David the crown and bracelet that belonged to Saul. David tore his clothes and mourned their deaths.

If you are bereaved, you have been robbed of something. Therefore, you can be in grief over more than the loss of a person. Maybe you lost your job, a relationship, or a pet.

Describe a loss you have experienced and its effect on your day-to-day activities.

Write a prayer giving the situation to God and asking him to strengthen you in your time of bereavement.

As you know, we are more affected by things than we are willing to admit. Grief robs you of your joy and reminds you of the hard facts about the world in which we live.

REACT: When you drop your kids off at school, do you weep like you'll never see them again? When you drop your spouse at the store and park the car, do you bid a final forever farewell? No. When you say "I'll see you soon," you mean it. When you stand in the cemetery and stare down at the soft, freshly turned earth, and promise "I'll see you soon," you speak truth. Reunion is a splinter of an eternal moment away.

There is no need for you to "to grieve like the rest of men, who have no hope" (1 Thessalonians 4:13 NIV).

So go ahead, face your grief. Give yourself time. Permit yourself tears. God understands. He knows the sorrow of a grave. He buried his son. But he also knows the joy of resurrection. And, by his power, you will too.

Based on what God taught me in this lesson, I will:

11

BLIND INTERSECTIONS

LESSON OBJECTIVE: To discover how God advises his followers and to commit to consulting God in times of decision

> It happened after this that David inquired of the LORD, saying, "Shall I go up to any of the cities of Judah?" (2 Samuel 2:1 NKJV)

REWIND: Maybe David had learned his lesson. He had tried making decisions without consulting God and things didn't turn out so well. He also had consulted God before making a decision and things went much better.

Describe a time when you have made a decision without consulting God. What was the end result?

Number the following steps in the order you normally employ them.

- ☐ Experience the consequences
- ☐ Analyze the situation
- ☐ Evaluate the options
- ☐ Consult God and his Word
- ☐ Seek godly counsel
- ☐ Make the decision

RETHINK: David wasted no time. He didn't try several things and then turn to God; he turned to God asking what he should do? David got his answer straight from God. Wouldn't it be nice to have God answer us directly? The good news is that he has pre-answered most of our questions either directly or in principle. We call it the Bible! The bad news is that most people don't take the time to know what the Bible says.

What keeps you from consulting God's Word when you are faced with a decision?

REFLECT: Read 2 Samuel 2:1–7. God had a plan that presupposed David's obedience. As if he was on auto-pilot, David turned to God and obeyed him. It's one thing to know what God expects; it's another thing to actually do it!

What is the ultimate outcome of knowing what God expects and choosing not to do it?

David became king over Judah. It had been a long time since that day in Bethlehem when he first was anointed by Samuel. A lot of things had happened.

Think back to the time when you first accepted Jesus as your Lord and Savior. There have been a lot of things that have happened since then. Describe a few key points in your spiritual journey.

REACT: You have a heart for God? Heed it. A family of faith? Consult it. A Bible? Read it. You have all you need to face the giant-sized questions of your life. Most of all, you have a God who loves you too much to let you wander.

God isn't playing hide and seek with you; he loves you and wants you to experience an abundant life.

Based on what God taught me in this lesson, I will:

12

STRONG HOLDS

Scriptural Focus: 2 Samuel 5:1–12

LESSON OBJECTIVE: To discover your strongholds and commit to trusting God to overcome them

So David went on and became great, and the LORD God of hosts was with him. (2 Samuel 5:10 NKJV)

REWIND: During the time that David ran from Saul, he often sought refuge in a stronghold. One such place was Masada, along the western shore of the Dead Sea. A stronghold was strong so it withstood assault and it had the ability to hold anyone or anything within its boundaries. From the outside, Jerusalem was such a place. Its walls and inhabitants were formidable. Yet Jerusalem was the city David needed in order to unite the tribes of Israel. Strongholds disintegrate when God shows up.

You might be living in a stronghold. Which of the following has a grip on you?

- ☐ my ego
- ☐ my job
- ☐ sex
- ☐ worry
- ☐ possessions
- ☐ other: _____

- ☐ my ambition
- ☐ a relationship
- ☐ pornography
- ☐ money
- ☐ personal appearance

RETHINK: To everyone else, attacking Jerusalem was a waste of time. Yet David saw it as a battle he could win.

What made David see something others didn't see?

REFLECT: Read 2 Samuel 5:1–12. The key term in this passage is *nevertheless*. It sets popular opinion against godly possibility. Take another look at verse 6.

What was popular opinion?

Think about your life. You've had some *nevertheless* moments, haven't you? You have had some times when it seemed everything was against you, but you persevered to achieve a goal. In the space provided below, list a few examples of your *nevertheless* moments.

Popular opinion said . . . nevertheless . . . this happened!

REACT: Peter stuck his foot in his mouth. Joseph was imprisoned in Egypt. The Samaritan woman had been married five times. Jesus was dead in the grave . . . Nevertheless: Peter preached, Joseph ruled, the woman shared, Jesus rose—and you? You fill in the blank. Your "nevertheless" awaits you.

Based on what God taught me in this lesson, I will:

13

DISTANT DEITY

Scriptural Focus: 2 Samuel 6:1–19

LESSON OBJECTIVE: To discover how we have made ordinary what God intends to be extraordinary and to commit to celebrating God's presence

> Then David danced before the LORD with all his might; and David was wearing a linen ephod. So David and all the house of Israel brought up the ark of the LORD with shouting and with the sound of the trumpet. (2 Samuel 6:14–15 NKJV)

REWIND: The ark of the covenant had fallen into the possession of the Philistines before being taken to the house of Abinadab. It seems the people of Israel had forgotten all about it until David came along and desired to move it to Jerusalem. The only problem was that David handled the ark in the same manner the Philistines handled it and, as a result, the laws regarding its movement were broken.

Has your reverence for God decayed to the point that you don't think much about it any more? Do you really understand God's holiness and tremble at the thought of being in his presence? Or has encountering God become nothing more than a social engagement that resembles a high school football game?

Use the scale below to rate your response to God's holiness.

Cold	Medium	Hot	Red Hot

RETHINK: When David moved the ark the first time, he did it in all the wrong ways and eventually called off the parade following the death of Uzzah.

Maybe you've never moved the ark, but has there been a time when you have been less than respectful of God's presence and priority? What response does God expect from you?

REFLECT: Read 2 Samuel 6:1–19. After three months, David resumed the movement of the ark and, this time, he did it the right way. As a result, he celebrated its arrival in Jerusalem with a joyous (and almost naked) dance. David was delighted to have God where he belonged.

Are there parts of your life that are off-limits to God? Do you see him as a cosmic killjoy who wants to stomp out a good time before it happens? If so, you misunderstand God and you misunderstand what it means to have a good time.

In the space below, write a note to God inviting him into any off-limits areas of your life. Be honest with him; he already knows the areas where he's not welcome. Be honest with yourself; ignoring the giant won't make it go away.

REACT: Uzzah's lifeless body cautions against irreverence. No awe of God leads to the death of man. God won't be cajoled, commanded, conjured up, or called down. He is a personal God who loves and heals and helps and intervenes. He doesn't respond to magic potions or clever slogans. He looks for more. He looks for reverence, obedience, and God-hungry hearts.

And when he sees them, he comes! And when he comes, let the band begin. And, yes, a reverent heart and a dancing foot can belong to the same person. David had both, do you?

Based on what God taught me in this lesson, I will:

14
TOUGH PROMISES

⟡

Scriptural Focus: 2 Samuel 9:1–13

LESSON OBJECTIVE: To discover how God keeps his promises and to resolve to keep our promises to God and others

So Mephibosheth dwelt in Jerusalem, for he ate continually at the king's table. And he was lame in both his feet. (2 Samuel 9:13 NKJV)

REWIND: Life for David was good. Saul was history, the ark was in its rightful place, and David finally was the ruler God said he would be. But David remembered a promise he made to Jonathan when he first began running from Saul. David promised Jonathan he would show kindness to him and, if he died, to Jonathan's family. It was time for David to keep his word.

Have you made promises in the heat of the moment that you struggled to keep when the heat was off? Which of the following statements have you made?

- ☐ God, if you get me out of this situation, I promise I'll read my Bible everyday.
- ☐ God, if you will just provide some way for me to pay this bill, I'll tithe the rest of my life.
- ☐ Honey, if you will forgive me just this time, I'll never do that again.
- ☐ other: _____

Promise-keeping might not be in style, but the degree to which you keep your promises reflects on your character and integrity.

If your promise-keeping reflects your character and integrity, what might be God's opinion of you?

God majors in promise-keeping. In fact, you will never find a promise he has broken or will ever break!

RETHINK: Mephibosheth was a special-needs child. He had been injured when his nurse was escaping the battle that killed his grandfather, Saul, and his father, Jonathan. Of course, medical technology then was non-existent, so Mephibosheth was crippled. He wasn't exactly the kind of person the king would take a liking to. But David remembered his promise to Jonathan.

Keeping some promises moves us out of our comfort zones. How might keeping the following promises make someone uncomfortable?

I will welcome all people into my home so that I can tell them about God.

I will do whatever it takes so that my family and friends experience a life-changing relationship with Jesus Christ.

I will not go anywhere or do anything that might cause someone to doubt my relationship with God.

REFLECT: Read 2 Samuel 9:1–13. David could easily have said, "I'm not aware of anyone in Jonathan's family who survived the battle, so my conscience is clean." But he wasn't looking for a way around the promise; he was looking for a way to make his promise good. He understood that a promise that is not kept is nothing but a lie.

Do you look for ways to quickly dismiss yourself from keeping the promises you've made? Do you often make promises just so you can experience immediate gratification?

Write in the space below a few of the promises you have made to God, your spouse, and/or your kids.

If the words above are true, you have some marching orders. If the words above aren't true, you need to have a conversation with God and those to whom you have lied. God keeps his promises because he has stubborn love. He isn't looking for an easy way around his promises; he is keeping them in spite of our unfaithfulness and doubts!

REACT: God calls on you to illustrate stubborn love. Incarnate fidelity. God is giving you a Mephibosheth-sized chance to show your children and your neighbors what real love does. Embrace it. Who knows? Someone may tell your story of loyalty to illustrate the loyalty of God.

Based on what God taught me in this lesson, I will:

15

THIN AIR-OGANCE

※

Scriptural Focus: 2 Samuel 11:1–17

LESSON OBJECTIVE: To discover God's attitude toward arrogance and to commit to a life of humility

> It happened in the spring of the year, at the time when kings go out to battle, that David sent Joab and his servants with him, and all Israel; and they destroyed the people of Ammon and besieged Rabbah. But David remained at Jerusalem. (2 Samuel 11:1 NKJV)

REWIND: There was the place David should have been—the battle—and the place he was—Jerusalem. This is the setting for one of the better-known stories about David. He wasn't where he should have been, so he wasn't doing what he should have been doing. Therefore, he did what he shouldn't have done in the place he didn't belong! Got that?

From David's palace he could see his kingdom and he also could see the home of Uriah and Bathsheba. Uriah was at war—where he belonged—and Bathsheba was on her rooftop bathing. Was this the customary place for bathing? Maybe. Was Bathsheba knowingly tempting David? Maybe. But what David did was David's fault. David wasn't a victim.

In a litigation-happy society we have developed the habit of claiming victim status when we really are responsible for our actions. When we burn our tongues on hot coffee, it's the restaurant's fault. When we lose our temper, it's the server's fault. When we bail on our responsibilities at home, it's the boss's fault.

Describe a time when you have blamed someone else for your bad decision.

Blame whomever you like, but you suffer the consequences for your actions and decisions. It might not be in style to accept personal responsibility, but if God doesn't hold other people responsible for your actions, what makes you think you can do it?

RETHINK: Everything was going great for David. His throne was secure, his people were prosperous, his approval rating was high, and as a result, his ego was inflated. He went from being the humble servant to being the demanding CEO of Israel. He sent and then he sinned!

Take a look back at the past week. What are some things you have done out of an over-inflated ego?

Who are some of the people who have been negatively affected by your egotistical actions?

Most people have a tough time being impressed with people who are over-impressed with themselves. Could people feel that way about you?

REFLECT: Read 2 Samuel 11:1–17. David let his ego get away from him. He did what kings didn't do; he sent his men to battle and stayed comfortably behind. Great leaders never ask anyone to do something they aren't willing to do themselves. David left his humility in the closet and put on his ego-coat. He ignored the warnings about Bathsheba—she's married, you know her husband, be careful. He ignored what he knew about God—he knows what you do even if no one else does, he holds you accountable for your actions. He ignored the character qualities in his own life and he did what he wanted to do with no regard for Bathsheba, Uriah, the kingdom, the consequences, or God.

You might be in the middle of a situation similar to that of David. Maybe it doesn't involve an inappropriate relationship. Maybe it does. It might involve business principles, moral compromises, bad habits, or careless self-gratification.

Describe the steps you should take to stop the situation before it's too late.

David's self-centeredness erupted into a murder plot and tragic consequences for him and his family. If David had considered the consequences, he might have reconsidered his actions. David's weakness overcame his power. His ego overcame his relationship with God. Is the same thing happening to you?

REACT: Do you think you are high and mighty? God has a cure for you—come down from the mountain. You'll be amazed what you hear and who you see. And you'll breathe a whole lot easier.

Based on what God taught me in this lesson, I will:

16

COLOSSAL COLLAPSES

Scriptural Focus: 2 Samuel 12:1–15

LESSON OBJECTIVE: To understand God's omniscience and to commit to respecting his holiness and his Word

So David said to Nathan, "I have sinned against the LORD." And Nathan said to David, "The LORD also has put away your sin; you shall not die." (2 Samuel 12:13 NKJV)

REWIND: David, David, David. Why? A man with everything doesn't need to rob someone else. Yet, that is what David did. He thought the cover-up worked. Uriah was "killed in action," he showed mercy to Bathsheba by marrying her, and no one knew what really happened. But David's conscience wouldn't be quiet. And God wouldn't keep quiet. He sent the prophet Nathan to confront David.

Is there something you have done or said that just won't go away? Is your conscience bothering you? Talk to God about it right now. Confess your sin to him and ask for his forgiveness.

David's sin with Bathsheba had far-reaching consequences. Review the story in 2 Samuel 11 and 12 and list in the space below the consequences of their sin.

Nathan's parable points out how easily it is for us to hold other people to higher standards than we live by. Think about the way you judge other people. How would you stand up against the same standards?

RETHINK: Nathan put his life in jeopardy when he told David that he was the subject of the parable. In other words, Nathan said, "Hey, king, I know what you did with Bathsheba . . . all of it!" Nathan was the spokesperson for God. God witnessed David's disobedience.

Why was it important for David to be reminded that God knew what had happened?

How do you feel knowing that God knows everything you have done and/or thought?

David confessed that his sin, though with Bathsheba, was against God. Do you see your sin in the same way?

REFLECT: Read 2 Samuel 12:1–15. Though David was forgiven, the consequences of his sin were not erased. David's home would never be the same. It is important to understand that forgiveness doesn't always prevent the consequences of our sin. Knowing that should change the process we go through when considering being disobedient to God.

Make a list of three or four steps you should use to make sure you don't willingly do something that is contrary to God's instructions.

List some people you can call on to help you be more accountable to God.

REACT: God did with David's sin what he does with yours and mine—he put it away. It's time for you to put your "third week of March, 1987," to rest. Assemble a meeting of three parties: you, God, and your memory. Place the mistake before the judgment seat of God. Let him condemn it, let him pardon it, and let him "put it away."

Based on what God taught me in this lesson, I will:

17

FAMILY MATTERS

✺

Scriptural Focus: 2 Samuel 15:13–14; 30–31

LESSON OBJECTIVE: To understand the value of one's family and to commit to giving your family the priority God expects

> So David went up by the Ascent of the Mount of Olives, and wept as he went up; and he had his head covered and went barefoot. And all the people who were with him covered their heads and went up, weeping as they went up. (2 Samuel 15:30 NKJV)

REWIND: A broken man ascended the Mount of Olives. For everything we know good about David, there is one flaw that screams loudly—David failed to make his family a priority. He was rich, popular, powerful, and attractive. He had the best house, chariots, sunglasses, and hair. By the world's standards—maybe by your standards—he was worthy of the cover of *People* magazine. Yet he shuffles up the Mount of Olives in mourning. What makes the powerful weep?

The powerful weep when they realize that what they've been chasing can't deliver what it promised. A rendezvous with a forbidden love plunged the king's house into turmoil. His collection of eight wives and countless other "loves" produced children he never prized. David's attention was everywhere except at home. Can you relate?

If you have twenty-four units of attention to give, how many of them are invested in your spouse, children, and home? _____

How many are invested in your job, social life, and outside interests? _____

How many are invested in the study of God's Word and prayer? _____

Based on your responses, to what degree are you like David? Explain your response.

It's easy to criticize David. After all, he had everything going for him so he had no excuse for neglecting his family. Neither do you!

RETHINK: David's escape from Jerusalem was the result of a coup by Absalom, one of his sons. While David's attention was diverted toward things that didn't matter, Absalom took over. Do you see the parallel?

What outside threats could sneak into your home and take over while your attention is diverted elsewhere?

What should you do to protect your home against these subtle invasions?

If David had anticipated the ultimate outcome of his self-centered behavior, he might have made some different choices along the way. What about you? Are today's bad choices the first step toward tragic consequences?

REFLECT: Read 2 Samuel 15:13–14; 30–31. Absalom fast-talked his way into the hearts of the people of Israel to the point that they were willing to side with him against his father, David. David had won battle after battle, but he runs from his son. As he runs, he is overcome with sadness for the situation. David probably asked himself a lot of "what if" questions.

Take a few moments and ask yourself some "what if" questions. What if I let my family become less and less important? What if I find the enticement of someone else more exciting than that of my spouse? What if I make promises to my kids that are seldom kept? What if I succeed in business but lose my home? What if I worry more about what other people think about me than about what my spouse and kids think of me?

What's really important to you? List your priorities in the space below. How satisfied with your list is God?

REACT: I suspect that David would have traded all his conquered crowns for the tender arms of a wife. But it was too late. He died in the care of a stranger because he made strangers out of his family. But it's not too late for you. Make your wife the object of your highest devotion. Make your husband the recipient of your deepest passion. Love the one who wears your ring. And cherish the children who share your name. Succeed at home first.

Based on what God taught me in this lesson, I will:

18

DASHED HOPES

Scriptural Focus: 1 Chronicles 28:1–10

LESSON OBJECTIVE: To discover how God enables his people to succeed in spite of their failure and commit to living in total dedication to God

> Then King David rose to his feet and said, "Hear me, my brethren, and my people: I had it in my heart to build a house of rest for the ark of the covenant of the LORD, and for the footstool of our God, and had made preparations to build it. But God said to me, 'You shall not build a house for My name, because you have been a man of war and have shed blood.'" (1 Chronicles 28:2–3 NKJV)

REWIND: David's past caught up with him. His hopes of building the temple were interrupted by God. The task of building the temple would be passed to Solomon and David would die without seeing the ark of the covenant in its permanent home. Isn't there forgiveness . . . restoration . . . hope for David?

Forgiveness doesn't cancel consequences. Disobedience to God is sin, and sin, though forgiven, has a lasting effect on us. Do you want to avoid the consequences of your sin? Then avoid the sin. Otherwise there is no guarantee you will escape the consequences, even though you experience forgiveness.

What does God want to do through your life?

These are your hopes . . . let's make sure they aren't dashed!

RETHINK: As David addressed the crowd, he could have been bitter. Instead, he seemingly reflects on his journey—from shepherd boy to king. He really had nothing to complain about.

Consider God's work in your life. Give a brief history of your journey. Where did it begin? What has God done in and around you?

What do you have to be thankful for?

REFLECT: Read 1 Chronicles 28:1–10. Nearing the end of his life, David explains to the people that God prevented him from building the temple. He even explains why God stopped the process. You see, God wanted it done a different way. David could have bulled his way forward and built a temple any-way, but he chose this time to listen to God and to obey him.

Think about your life. Describe a time when you have gotten ahead of God and done something in spite of your understanding that God didn't want you to do it.

What were the consequences of getting ahead of God?

REACT: What do you do with the "but God" moments in life? When God interrupts your good plans, how do you respond? Will you let your "but God" moments become "yet God" opportunities?

Based on what God taught me in this lesson, I will:

19
TAKE GOLIATH DOWN!

Scriptural Focus: 1 Samuel 17:32–51

LESSON OBJECTIVE: To remember how weak our giants are in light of God's strength and to commit to trusting God to strengthen us with his power

> Then he took his staff in his hand; and he chose for himself five smooth stones from the brook, and he put them in a shepherd's bag, in a pouch which he had, and his sling was in his hand. And he drew near to the Philistine. (1 Samuel 17:40 NKJV)

REWIND: The nay-sayers were plenty. How could this shepherd boy stand against Goliath? The boy was so small he couldn't move wearing Saul's armor. So, he went back to being what he was—a shepherd with a staff. The only addition was the five smooth stones he collected from the brook. Boys don't defeat giants; shepherds don't defeat warriors. David knew he couldn't win this battle. But he knew God could . . . and would!

Your giants taunt you reminding you of their power and might. You can't win. You're born to lose. What can you say in response to your giants?

It's not mind over matter; it's God over giants!

RETHINK: Five stones. A boy. A sling. Your equipment for the battle might be much different. A young lady. Godly principles. Determination. A businessman. Marital vows. A solid commitment. When you compare your resources against the power of the giants, you can easily become pessimistic about your chances of winning. But you have the Creator of the universe on your side.

What weapons do you have to fight your giants? What are some things you do to keep yourself spiritually prepared for the battle?

REFLECT: Read 1 Samuel 17:32–51. No one gave David a chance against Goliath. Five stones or five hundred boulders—it didn't really matter. If five stones would have done it, Goliath would have been history long ago. But it wasn't the stones!

What was it that made it possible for David to go into battle against Goliath with such confidence?

What keeps you from having this type of confidence when you face your giants?

REACT: Why did David quarry a quintet of stones? Could it be because Goliath had four brothers the size of tyrannosaurus rexes? For all David knew, they'd come running over the hill to defend their brother. David was ready to empty the chamber, if that's what it took. Imitate him. Never give up. One prayer might not be enough. One apology might not do it. One day or month of resolve might not suffice. You may get knocked down a time or two . . . but don't quit. Keep loading the rocks. Keep swinging the sling. David took five stones. He made five decisions. Do likewise. Consider: Past. Prayer. Priority. Passion. And persistence.

Next time Goliath wakes you up, reach for a stone. Odds are he'll be out of the room before you can load your sling.

Based on what God taught me in this lesson, I will:

SMALL GROUP LEADER GUIDES
SMALL GROUP SESSION 1

LESSON OBJECTIVE: To discover how problems affect our lives and commit to trusting God to overcome them

Before the small group session read Chapter 1 of *Facing Your Giants*.

Scriptural Focus: 1 Samuel 17:1–11

THE CONTEXT: Goliath had been taunting the Israelite army from a mountain across the valley. Though Saul was the military leader of the nation, he refused to engage Goliath in battle. David's three oldest brothers were part of Saul's army, so Jesse—David's father—sent bread and grain to his oldest sons by way of young David. Upon arriving at the camp, David hears the taunts of Goliath and decides to take action.

GETTING STARTED: Enlist a volunteer to read aloud 1 Samuel 17:1–11. Take a few minutes to establish the context for this passage.

DISCOVERING THE TRUTH: Distribute note cards and instruct students to list on the cards one "giant" they are facing. Collect the cards and shuffle them so that no one's identity is revealed. Hold the cards for use later in the session.

TERRIFIED BY TAUNTS: As long as the Israelites were terrified, Goliath had the battle won. He never used his spear or swung his fist—he didn't have to! The Israelites weren't about to engage in a battle they knew they couldn't win. Goliath's taunts just reminded them of their weaknesses and kept them in bondage to their nemesis.

Hopelessness is a frustrating place to live. Yet many people choose to let their giants keep them fenced in with no hope for escape. Why is it so hard for people to face their giants?

PARALYZED BY FEAR: The Israelites were paralyzed because the situation looked hopeless. In what ways are you paralyzed by the hopelessness of your situation? When you analyze your situation, are you more like Saul or David?

FREED BY FAITH: David's approach was different—he chose to pay little attention to the giant and to put his focus on God. David already had seen God at work in his life. He knew God had intervened in hopeless situations before, and he was certain God would intervene this time. The size of the enemy doesn't matter from God's perspective.

What are some things you can do to refocus away from the giants and toward God? What might be the end result of a God-focused life?

MAKING IT REAL: Take the cards you collected earlier in the session and read aloud the "giants" that have been listed. After reading each card, tear it in half signifying its powerlessness in light of God's power. Close in prayer asking God to give each person the strength he or she needs to face the giants.

SMALL GROUP SESSION 2

⌘

LESSON OBJECTIVE: To discover the qualities that led to David's becoming king and commit to developing those qualities in our lives

Before the small group session read Chapter 2 of *Facing Your Giants.*

Scriptural Focus: 1 Samuel 16:1–13

THE CONTEXT: Because the people desired a king, God instructed Samuel to anoint Saul. It wasn't long before Saul started pursuing his own desires rather than pleasing God. Little by little, his focus on God was replaced by a focus on himself. This, of course, angered God. As a result, God rejected Saul as king and removed his spirit from Saul's life. God, therefore, assigned Samuel the task of anointing Saul's successor—a task that was uncommon while the predecessor was still alive.

GETTING STARTED: Enlist a volunteer to read aloud 1 Samuel 16:1–13. Take a few minutes to establish the context for this passage.

DISCOVERING THE TRUTH: Make a two-column chart on the board and label the first column "Man looks at . . ." and the second column "but God looks at . . ." As you work through the main points below, fill in the chart with qualities that man says are important and the qualities that God says are important.

A PUZZLING PROCESS: As Jesse presented his boys for Samuel's consideration, it became clear that the process would be more involved than Samuel imagined. Like many of us, Samuel looked first at the outward appearance only to be told by God that looks don't matter. In what ways are we like Samuel when it comes to evaluating ourselves and others for use by God?

A DIFFERENT CRITERIA: Even Samuel expected one of Jesse's older sons to be picked by God, but Jesse's first seven sons were eliminated from consideration because they lacked the qualities a godly king needed. Review the list of qualities that are important to God and discuss why it is so hard to develop those qualities in our lives.

A HIGHER CALLING: Samuel was sure he understood God's instructions—God had selected one of Jesse's sons to be king. The only son Samuel had not seen was David, the least likely of the eight brothers. What made David God's choice? David had qualities the human eye couldn't see. In today's world, many people spend a great deal of time and money trying to perfect those things that are visible. What are some things we can do to strengthen the inner qualities that are important to God?

MAKING IT REAL: Review the list of items on the board and call attention to the qualities that man thinks are important. Discuss some ways to make those characteristics less important and the characteristics in the second column more important. Close in prayer asking God to give everyone present the wisdom to see themselves and others from God's perspective.

SMALL GROUP SESSION 3

⁍

LESSON OBJECTIVE: To discover how God is faithful to those who trust and obey him and commit to a lifestyle of obedience to God

Before the small group session read Chapter 3 of *Facing Your Giants*.

Scriptural Focus: 1 Samuel 18:1–16

THE CONTEXT: Goliath was dead. David was carrying around the giant's head as a souvenir and proof that Goliath's taunts had been permanently silenced. All the people were happy—that is, all the people except Saul! As the Philistines vacated their camp, the Israelites moved in and looted their tents. This was all the more reason to celebrate David's triumph and all the more reason for insecurity to consume Saul. When David returned to the Israelite camp, Saul demanded an audience and asked David to identify his father.

GETTING STARTED: Enlist a volunteer to read aloud 1 Samuel 18:1–16. Take a few minutes to establish the context for this passage.

DISCOVERING THE TRUTH: As you review this lesson in the study guide, use the following information and questions to help make the session applicable to the lives of the individuals in the class.

MISSION ACCOMPLISHED: The Philistines had been a problem for the Israelites for as long as they had inhabited Canaan. Ridding themselves of the Philistine threat was a desire, but in the minds of the people, it was impossible. The Philistines were superior warriors with superior weapons and, to beat all, they physically had been super-sized! It was the chihuahua versus the Great Dane! When the Great Dane growled, the chihuahua trembled. David's unlikely victory over Goliath was reason to celebrate. What unlikely spiritual victories have you experienced? How does remembering those victories affect your faith in God?

A JEALOUS MANIAC: Saul wouldn't go into battle against Goliath, but when Goliath was dead, Saul wanted the credit. Rather than focus on the collective victory, Saul centered on the personal loss. Read 1 Samuel 18:6–9 and note Saul's attitude toward David. Call for volunteers to summarize Saul's attitude in one or two words. List responses on the board. When something good happens why do some people celebrate and others become jealous?

DESPERATION REALIZED: 1 Samuel 18:12 says that Saul was afraid of David, yet David posed no physical threat to Saul. David was a threat to Saul's ego and that, to Saul, was a much more dangerous threat! Of course, David was God's anointed king, so nothing was going to happen to David apart from what God allowed. Twice in this passage, we see David's behavior characterized in the same way. Call for a volunteer to read aloud 1 Samuel 18:5 and 18:14. What phrase is common?

MAKING IT REAL: Behaving wisely means acting in ways that are consistent with God's character. Part of the action-consequence cycle is *behave wisely*—God is with you. You can look at it a couple of ways. Because God is with you, you behave wisely or you behave wisely and God continues to be with you. The bottom line is that behaving wisely is directly connected to one's relationship with God. Discuss ways to discover the truth about God's character and ways to make it real in your daily life. Pray, asking God to give you all wisdom as you seek to please him each day.

SMALL GROUP SESSION 4

꧁ᛝ꧂

LESSON OBJECTIVE: To realize how God sustains us even when we are desperate and to commit to trusting God through the good times and the bad

Before the small group session read Chapter 4 of *Facing Your Giants*.

Scriptural Focus: 1 Samuel 21:1–9

THE CONTEXT: Jonathan's loyalty to David exceeded his loyalty to Saul. David sensed Saul wanted to kill him, but Jonathan didn't believe it. So they came up with a plan that would ensure David's safety. David went into a field and awaited a sign from Jonathan. Jonathan, when questioned about David's absence from the king's table, said that he had given David permission to return to Bethlehem for a sacrifice with his family. The news angered Saul so much that he threw a spear at his son. This was confirmation for Jonathan that David was in great danger. So he went into the field and gave David the signal to run. After telling Jonathan goodbye, David headed for Nob, a small town on the outskirts of Jerusalem occupied by the priests who had been displaced from Shiloh. There he met Ahimelech, one of the priests. Ahimelech raised the red flag when he encountered David all alone. So he asked some questions. That's when David decided that telling the truth was optional.

GETTING STARTED: Enlist a volunteer to read aloud 1 Samuel 21:1–9. Take a few minutes to establish the context for this passage.

DISCOVERING THE TRUTH: As you review this lesson in the study guide, use the following information and questions to help make the session applicable to the lives of the individuals in the class.

COVERED TRACKS: David was running for his life, yet when Ahimelech approached him he acted as if everything was fine; he was simply carrying out a "top priority" mission. Discuss how people often act like David when responding to "How are you doing?" What keeps people from being honest about their circumstances and feelings?

A REQUEST FOR BREAD: Even though the bread had been set aside for religious purposes, David argued that the bread had been replaced with fresh bread so it was no longer consecrated bread. So, Ahimelech gave David the bread. David manipulated the law for personal benefit. In what ways are we tempted to manipulate God's Word in order to achieve selfish goals?

ONE MORE THING: This is the same David who defeated Goliath and cut off his head. Goliath's sword had become property of the priests at Nob. Whereas David in the past relied solely on God to defeat his enemies, he now looks to the priest for a weapon. David once had stood in the valley and shouted to Goliath that God's power was stronger than the sword he bore. Now David takes that same sword, saying "there is none like it." Undoubtedly, God would have met David's need without David lying. God knew the truth; it was David who seemed to have a problem with it! When times get tough, to what are you likely to turn before turning to God? What would be the benefit of turning to God when trouble first appeared?

MAKING IT REAL: David lost his focus. When trouble came looking for him, he left, he lied, and he languished. When he left Jerusalem, he left behind more than the city; he left behind his total trust in God. Once he stopped depending on God, he found lying much easier. Once he started lying, he reinterpreted God's instructions for personal gain. Once he redefined truth, he started trusting in himself more than in God. It was a vicious cycle that wasn't limited to David. Many people today still follow David's path to futility.

Close in prayer asking God to enable his people to trust him more as they encounter difficulties in life.

SMALL GROUP SESSION 5

LESSON OBJECTIVE: To discover God's presence in the midst of personal struggles and commit to look for God's encouragement in the people he brings into our lives

Before the small group session read Chapter 5 of *Facing Your Giants*.

Scriptural Focus: 1 Samuel 21:10–22:5

THE CONTEXT: Having successfully lied to get food and a weapon, David left Nob and headed for Gath. Gath was one of the major Philistine cities and had been the home to Goliath and his family. Because Gath bordered the Israelite territory, it had been instrumental in the ongoing conflict between the Israelites and the Philistines. Because he had slain Goliath, David knew he wouldn't be welcomed as a hero. In fact, David was concerned about his safety in the city.

GETTING STARTED: Enlist a volunteer to read aloud 1 Samuel 21:10–22:5. Take a few minutes to establish the context for this passage.

DISCOVERING THE TRUTH: As you review this lesson in the study guide, use the following information and questions to help make the session applicable to the lives of the individuals in the class.

FAKING IT: In the past, David had relied on God to sustain him through the difficulties he faced. Now David resorts to lying and acting to achieve his objectives. He acted insane causing King Achish to order David away thereby saving David's life. What were David's choices in this situation? What does his choice to fake insanity say about his faith in God? In what ways are you tempted to solve your problems rather than trust God to work them out?

MAKING IT: David had visited two cities—Nob and Gath. In both situations he misrepresented the truth and fled quickly. David's integrity was sliding downhill so he headed for a cave—a place where he would have no one to lie to. David's family heard about his encampment in the cave and decided to join him there. Not only did his family join him, but all of the misfits and rebels who sought refuge from Saul met him there. Just when David was settling in for a nice pity party, he found himself surrounded by people just like him.

Think about a time in your life when God has used your experiences to enable you to meet the needs of someone going through a similar situation. Was your focus shifted from self to others? If so, what was the end result for you and the others God brought into your life?

RESTORING IT: David's recent track record wasn't great. He had abandoned the vibrant faith in God that delivered Goliath into his hands. He had abandoned the childlike faith that enabled him to kill bears while protecting his sheep. He forgot all about God's track record of faithfulness and power. So God brought a prophet to help David refocus on him. Gad told David to go to Judah, and David did as he was told. Maybe being around a godly person reminded David what it was like to be that close to God. Whatever happened, it refocused David toward God's plan and he abandoned his personal pursuit and started listening to God again.

God has a way of bringing people into our lives to help us refocus on what's important. Think about a time when you strayed from God. Who did God use to help bring you back into a right relationship with him? What do you do to maintain that level of relationship with God?

MAKING IT REAL: It had been a long road. When David ran, he left behind his dependence on God and started taking matters into his own hands. The more he did it, the worse things got. Seeking time alone, he found himself surrounded by people just like him—desperate and on the run. Maybe you are on the run today. It's time to let all of God's misfits band together to accomplish great things. If God only used perfect people, he would have only had one choice throughout all of history! Close in prayer asking God to help you focus on his purposes especially when the situation seems hopeless.

SMALL GROUP SESSION 6

LESSON OBJECTIVE: To discover God's grace and commit to extending that grace to everyone we encounter

Before the small group session read Chapter 6 of *Facing Your Giants*.

Scriptural Focus: 1 Samuel 24:1–15

THE CONTEXT: With Saul on his trail, David moves throughout the territory just outside of Jerusalem. He hid in caves, hills, and cities while pondering what he had done to deserve Saul's wrath. Meanwhile, Saul made it a point to extract information from everyone he could and to kill anyone suspected of offering help to David. David ran to Keilah, a fortified city that was under attack by the Philistines. God instructed David to assist the people of Keilah in their battle. At first, David's men rejected the idea. But after consulting with God a second time, David and his men fought and defeated the Philistines. But David wasn't secure there. God told him that Saul was on the way and that the people of Keilah would hand him over to Saul. Therefore David and his men left the city and headed for the wilderness of Ziph.

The Ziphites were no help to David. They twice revealed to Saul where David was hiding. As a result, David and his men fled to the Wilderness of Maon. There David occupied one mountain and Saul another. But David and his men were outnumbered. Saul's army began to encircle David's camp trapping David on the mountain. Things looked hopeless. At the end of 1 Samuel 23, a messenger informed Saul that the Philistines had invaded the land, so Saul called off the pursuit of David in order to defend the nation against the Philistines. With Saul's attention diverted, David and his men escaped to En Gedi on the western shore of the Dead Sea.

GETTING STARTED: Enlist a volunteer to read aloud 1 Samuel 24:1–15. Take a few minutes to establish the context for this passage.

DISCOVERING THE TRUTH: As you review this lesson in the study guide, use the following information and questions to help make the session applicable to the lives of the individuals in the class.

RELENTLESS PURSUIT: Saul wasn't about to give up. He had pursued David all the way to En Gedi, north of Masada along the western side of the Dead Sea. The Bible describes in detail the events that transpired. David and his men sought safety in a cave—the same cave into which Saul went to "relieve himself." It was David's chance to end Saul's reign and take the throne. Saul was alone, unaware of David's presence. The pursuer became the pursued . . . or so it seems.

Ask volunteers to describe a time when God has given them an opportunity for revenge against someone who was the source of grief and difficulty in their lives. How did they respond?

RELENTLESS GRACE: David's men encouraged him to strike Saul, but David refused. Instead, he cut off a piece of Saul's robe and held it for safekeeping. If anyone had a reason to be mad, David did. Yet, as Saul leaves the cave, David approaches him, calls him by name, and displays the piece of Saul's robe he cut off. In effect, David said, "Hey Saul, if I was as mean as you, you would be dead right now." It was a wakeup call for Saul. He understood how merciful David had been to him in spite of his ill will toward David.

Ask volunteers to tell when they have been the recipient of unwarranted grace? How did it make you feel?

Grace often isn't realized until after the fact. We sometimes say, "This could have happened, but instead, this happened." If the end result was better than the original possibility, you experienced grace. Of course, the ultimate expression of grace came in the form of Jesus Christ who died so that you and I don't have to pay the penalty for our sin. I could have spent eternity separated from God in a real place called hell, but instead, I asked Jesus Christ to be my personal Savior so that I now will spend eternity in heaven. That is the ultimate example of grace!

A CHANGE OF HEART: Saul understood grace when he experienced grace, and experienced grace usually leads to a change of heart. You can't encounter God's love and walk away unchanged. You will be hardened and turn away from God or you will be drawn to him. Saul was drawn to God and changed. Not only did he give up his pursuit of David, but he asked David for mercy when David became king. Only God can accomplish change like that! Ask your small group: In what ways have you been changed by God's love? How does your relationship with God affect your relationships with other people?

MAKING IT REAL: David struggled like all of us. He had moments of spiritual brilliance that were countered by moments of selfish control. In the end, his understanding of grace allowed him to show mercy to his adversary and, as a result, change that adversary's life forever. Close in prayer asking God to help you show grace and mercy to those who seek to do you harm so that they might see God's love in a new way.

SMALL GROUP SESSION 7

⟨⟩

LESSON OBJECTIVE: To discover how one's commitment to God can overcome that person's self-centeredness

Before the small group session read Chapter 7 of *Facing Your Giants*.

Scriptural Focus: 1 Samuel 25:14–38

THE CONTEXT: Fresh off of his close encounter with Saul and an agreement that David would let Saul's descendents live, Saul went home and David returned to his stronghold just south of En Gedi. David and his men left for the Wilderness of Paran. There David encountered Nabal whose name meant "fool." Nabal took "egotistical" to a new level! He had everything that was supposed to make him a somebody, but the only thing Nabal really had going for him was his wife, Abigail. She was beautiful and possessed good judgment. (Remember, back then the girl didn't have a lot of say-so when it came to getting married!)

David and his men had defended the people of Maon and were well-respected by everyone except Nabal. Nabal had respect for no one other than himself. So Nabal planned a feast and began making preparations. David heard about it and sent ten men to request food. Nabal not only said no, he showed no respect for David or his contribution to the area's safety. So when David's men returned with Nabal's answer, David wasn't happy. He organized two-thirds of his men—leaving two hundred behind to guard the supplies—and he headed off to take care of Nabal once and for all.

GETTING STARTED: Enlist one or more volunteers to read aloud 1 Samuel 25:14–38. Take a few minutes to establish the context for this passage.

DISCOVERING THE TRUTH: As you review this lesson in the study guide, use the following information and questions to help make the session applicable to the lives of the individuals in the class.

DANGER ON THE HORIZON: David had no doubt that he and his men could easily defeat Nabal and his men. Apparently Abigail, Nabal's wife, agreed with David. Having been advised of David's plan to kill Nabal, Abigail gathered together the food David needed, loaded it on donkeys, and went out to meet David. Think back to the time when you first accepted Jesus Christ as your Lord and Savior. What danger was averted? How did you feel after your salvation experience?

A QUICK INTERVENTION: With two hundred loaves of bread, two skins of wine, five sheep ready for roasting, grain, raisins, and fig cakes, Abigail meets David's men. Now, David's men had been in the woods for quite a while and probably hadn't seen many women the likes of Abigail. Her beauty stopped them in their tracks. What has God used to stop you in your tracks? What danger was averted by your being stopped?

As Abigail approached David, she presented herself with humility and begged David to let her take the punishment for Nabal's actions. She saw the situation with spiritual eyes and reminded David that once he had been pursued and God had spared him from Saul's sword.

It is easy to see things from only one perspective. When David was being pursued, he wondered why. Now he was pursuing a man who was clueless about anything other than personal gratification. It took Abigail to remind David of God's plans for him.

JUDGMENT AVERTED: David listened to Abigail and confessed that he was about to make a big mistake. He sent Abigail on her way, and he and his men returned with the food Abigail provided. But the story doesn't end there. When Abigail returned to Nabal and told him that he had just been spared his life, Nabal suffered a heart attack and died. His death was credited to God, not David.

Taking God's place can be dangerous. In the end, Nabal was dead. But David didn't have Nabal's blood on his hands. When things are left to God they usually become less messy! In what ways have you been tempted to take control and do for God what he might do in his own time? What was the result of your actions?

MAKING IT REAL: By law, David might have had the right to kill Nabal. Yet God used Abigail to stop him. When we are headed for disobedience God often puts someone in our paths to redirect us and bring us to our senses. Pray, thanking God for the intervention he brings to our lives and ask for wisdom to listen to those God is using to guide us.

SMALL GROUP SESSION 8

✦

LESSON OBJECTIVE: To learn the warning signs of spiritual weariness and to commit to focusing on your relationship to God

Before the small group session read Chapter 8 of *Facing Your Giants*.

Scriptural Focus: 1 Samuel 27:1–4; 30:1–6

THE CONTEXT: Upon hearing of his close encounter with David, Nabal suffered a heart attack and died, leaving the beautiful and intelligent Abigail widowed. So David proposed to Abigail and also Ahinoam, taking both women as his wives. Earlier David had spared Saul's life in the cave and, as a result, Saul called off his hunt, leaving David safe. But egotistical people seldom call off the hunt for those whom they see as threats. When Saul was told that David was in the Wilderness of Ziph, he went there and resumed his pursuit. David suspected Saul was back, so he sent spies out to verify the threat. Upon their return and confirmation of Saul's presence, David went into Saul's camp under the cover of darkness and took Saul's spear and water jug, but not his life. Once again, David showed tangible proof that he had been merciful to Saul. Again Saul repents and returns home. But David isn't convinced he's seen the end of Saul. Weary from running, David makes a series of bad choices beginning with the decision to seek refuge with the Philistines.

GETTING STARTED: Enlist one or more volunteers to read aloud 1 Samuel 27:1–4 and 1 Samuel 30:1–6. Take a few minutes to establish the context for these passages.

DISCOVERING THE TRUTH: As you review this lesson in the study guide, use the following information and questions to help make the session applicable to the lives of the individuals in the class.

A DANGEROUS ALLEGIANCE: David lost hope and made a bad decision in order to escape Saul once and for all. The Philistines were enemy number one, but that didn't stop David from running to them. When David lost sight of God's perspective, he made decisions based on his personal view, even though he had witnessed first-hand God's power over his circumstances. Describe a time when you lost sight of God's perspective and made the mistake of trusting your own judgment. What was the outcome of that situation?

A SURPRISE ATTACK: With David and his men at Aphek preparing to do battle against the Israelites, his base camp at Ziklag was vulnerable. The Amalekites attacked Ziklag, burned the town, and took all of the women and children captive. Meanwhile, back at Aphek, David and his men were rejected by the Philistine princes and sent home.

David's escape to the enemy was tragic for his home and his family. The same is true today. Your escape will be evident in your home. While your attention is diverted, someone or something will sneak in and wreak havoc on those you say are the most important in your life. Like David, you might not discover the danger until it is too late.

What are some things that have become more important to you than your home? What unknown enemy is making its way into your home while you play army with your enemy?

David lost hope and as a result, lost his home, his family, and his reputation. Even his own men considered killing him because of the losses they suffered when Ziklag was attacked.

A CORRECT DECISION: Losing hope and deciding to do something that violated his calling began a downward spiral for David. Had he known what was going to happen, he probably would have reconsidered his decision to partner with the Philistines. Undoing the damage was impossible. Personal tragedy often leads to spiritual renewal. That's what happened with David.

With his family in captivity, his home burned, and his men threatening to kill him, David turned to God and strengthened himself.

How bad does life have to get before you turn back to God? What will you have to lose before you lay yourself bare before him and ask for his forgiveness and mercy? What are you losing right now because your attention is diverted away from God?

MAKING IT REAL: Could David's crisis have been avoided? Can your future crises be avoided by a continued focus on God? We can't be sure. Sometimes God uses negative situations in our lives to help others see his power. At other times we simply must live through the consequences of our bad decisions. Pray, asking God for wisdom and discernment so that the decisions you make will be in accordance with his desires for your life.

SMALL GROUP SESSION 9

❦

LESSON OBJECTIVE: To develop an awareness of God's providence and to commit to honoring others in accordance with God's attitude toward us

Before the small group session read Chapter 9 of *Facing Your Giants*.

Scriptural Focus: 1 Samuel 30:7–25

THE CONTEXT: After being kicked out of the Philistine army, David and his men returned to their base at Ziklag only to discover that the Amalekites had raided the town, plundered it, taken the women and children captive, and then burned what was left behind. David's wives, Abigail and Ahinoam, were among those taken captive. David's men looked for someone to blame, and they looked no farther than David. David looked to God and said (my paraphrase), "What's up with this?"

David then called for Abiathar, the priest and the son of the slain Ahimelech. Using the ephod—a holy garment used when seeking a word from God—David asked God if he should pursue the Amalekites. God told David that he should and that he would recover everyone and everything that had been taken from Ziklag. So David and his men pursued the Amalekites even though they were unsure where they were. Their first stop was about fifteen miles south at Brook Besor. There two hundred of David's men stayed to rest while the other four hundred continued after the Amalekites. With the help of an Egyptian servant left behind by the Amalekites, David and his men located and defeated their enemy and recovered everything, just as God had promised.

GETTING STARTED: Enlist one or more volunteers to read aloud 1 Samuel 30:7–25. Take a few minutes to establish the context for this passage.

DISCOVERING THE TRUTH: As you review this lesson in the study guide, use the following information and questions to help make the session applicable to the lives of the individuals in the class.

OBEDIENCE FINALLY: David's track record hadn't been so good. He took matters into his own hands and made a pretty big mess of things. With his family in captivity, his army on the verge of mutiny, and his home reduced to cinders, David turned to God.

What was the last thing that happened that forced you to turn to God in desperation?

Once David had God's instructions, he gathered his army and did what God said. What made following God such an easy choice for David this time? What motivates you to listen to God's instructions?

A DIVIDED ARMY: About fifteen miles south of Ziklag was the Brook Besor. David and his men paused there to refresh themselves. But when David rounded up his men to continue the pursuit, one-third of them refused to leave. Resting by the brook was too enticing. Have you been in a leadership position and decided to take some time off to rest? How long have you been resting? Are you doing what you want to do or are you resting out of obedience to God?

Rather than coerce resting soldiers into battle, David took those willing to fight and tracked down the Amalekites, attacked them, and recovered the people and property that belonged to them. Could the battle have been easier with all six hundred men? Probably. Was God's promised outcome affected because some men refused to fight? No!

Those who were resting missed out on the joy of the victory. Sure they heard about it, but they weren't there to see the faces of their family members when they were rescued. They weren't there to witness God's activity first hand. To them, the victory was just a story.

Do you overestimate your importance in God's work? God will accomplish his purposes with two-thirds of the people available and, in the end, it's those who are involved in what God is doing who will witness his power first hand.

A Collective Victory: Four hundred men went to battle and two hundred stayed behind at the brook. Who won? As far as David is concerned, they all did! David saw the battle as God's battle and the victory as God's victory. Those men who fought thought differently. They wanted to withhold from the resting soldiers the spoils of the victory.

In your attitude toward those who are "sitting by the brook" are you more like David's men or like David? Why?

David brought dignity to the resting men by claiming that they stayed behind with the supplies. They were "behind the scenes" people. When God wins, all of his people win, not just those who were frontline warriors.

In what ways are you honoring and encouraging the "behind the scenes" people in your workplace and/or church?

Making It Real: There are plenty of people who are on the front lines playing key roles in the things God is doing. There are others who have laid the foundation for the present work and now are resting. Still others are content to let everyone else do the work while they sit by the brook permanently. Pray, asking God to help you see your role in his work and commit to doing whatever it is he asks you to do.

SMALL GROUP SESSION 10

⌁

LESSON OBJECTIVE: To discover how grief affects us and to commit to trusting God in times of grief

Before the small group session read Chapter 10 of *Facing Your Giants*.

Scriptural Focus: 2 Samuel 1:4–12

THE CONTEXT: When we last encountered the Philistines and Israelites, they were lined up preparing for battle. It was during that preparation time that David and his men were dismissed from the Philistine army and sent back to Ziklag where they discovered the Amalekite invasion. Now let's pick up the story of the battle. The Philistines captured a majority of the Israelite army at Mount Gilboa and continued their pursuit of Saul and his sons. We have heard a lot about Jonathan, but Saul also had three other sons—Abinadab, Malchishua, and Ishbosheth. Apparently Ishbosheth was not in the company of Saul and his other sons because he was declared king after the deaths of the others. The Philistines already had killed Saul's three sons who were with him—including Jonathan—and Saul was injured in the battle.

Saul saw no hope, so he told his armor bearer to kill him, but the armor bearer refused. So Saul took his sword and fell on it, killing himself. The remaining Israelites fled and the Philistines took control of the territory. The men of Jabesh Gilead retrieved the bodies of Saul and his sons and buried them at Jabesh.

GETTING STARTED: Enlist one or more volunteers to read aloud 2 Samuel 1:4–12. Take a few minutes to establish the context for this passage.

DISCOVERING THE TRUTH: As you review this lesson in the study guide, use the following information and questions to help make the session applicable to the lives of the individuals in the class.

AN HONEST CONCERN: David had every reason to dismiss Saul from his mind. After all, Saul had lied to David and tried to kill him. Saul had been a source of trouble for longer than David wanted to remember. And Jonathan? David hadn't seen him in a while and, honestly, there were bigger things David had to deal with. But David showed genuine concern for Saul and Jonathan.

Who is someone God keeps bringing to your mind? How can you show concern for that person like David was concerned for Saul and Jonathan?

David wasn't looking for bad news; he honestly wanted Saul and Jonathan to be alive. After all Saul had done, David still gave him the honor due God's appointed leader. What should be your attitude toward the leaders God places in your life?

THE HORRIBLE TRUTH: The Amalekite messenger not only had bad news, he had proof that he was telling the truth. Saul and Jonathan were dead, the Israelites had retreated, and the Philistines had won. Welcome to your kingdom, David! When bad news comes your way, what is your attitude toward God and other people?

David didn't want to believe what he was hearing, but he had no choice. Saul would never again pursue him, but David found little comfort in that fact.

THE HEARTFELT REACTION: David entered a period of mourning for Saul, Jonathan, and the nation. David saw things differently. It wasn't all about him. David wrote a song about the occasion and ordered that it be taught to all generations.

Do you hide your feelings about things that matter to God? Do you mourn the things that God mourns, despise the things he despises, and love the things he loves? If not, you need to carefully evaluate your relationship with him. Rather than making God into something you are comfortable with, it's time to make you into something that looks more and more like God.

MAKING IT REAL: Grief and mourning are a part of life. It is one of those things we just have to work through. That's the key: through! Grief is not a final destination. It is not a place we should settle. It is a temporary condition related to an earthbound truth. Pray that God will strengthen you through your grief and enable you to be used to minister to those who are grieving.

SMALL GROUP SESSION 11

LESSON OBJECTIVE: To discover how God advises his followers and to commit to consulting God in times of decision

Before the small group session read Chapter 11 of *Facing Your Giants*.

Scriptural Focus: 2 Samuel 2:1–7

THE CONTEXT: With Saul and Jonathan dead, David pondered his future. After all, he had spent a great deal of time simply running from Saul, so his career had never really taken shape. Certainly he thought back to that day in Bethlehem when he was selected from among Jesse's boys to be the king. He remembered being anointed by Samuel. He reflected on everything he had been told. But he wanted to be sure. He ended his period of mourning and sought God's direction in his life.

GETTING STARTED: Enlist a volunteer to read aloud 2 Samuel 2:1–7. Take a few minutes to establish the context for this passage.

DISCOVERING THE TRUTH: As you review this lesson in the study guide, use the following information and questions to help make the session applicable to the lives of the individuals in the class.

WHAT SHOULD I DO? As was his custom, David went to God asking what he should do. He was directed to Hebron, a town twenty miles south of Jerusalem. Because of its location, it would make for a secure capital for

David's kingdom. How do you know what God wants you to do? Do you ever limit the options to only those things you want to do? Why?

IMMEDIATE OBEDIENCE: David didn't delay. He gathered his wives and his men and went to the place God said to go. The Bible tells us they dwelt there. What are some things you believe God wants you to do but you have not yet done? Why are you delaying your obedience?

GOD'S PLAN FULFILLED: David being anointed king over Judah should have come as no surprise. He had been told he would be king. God has a way of keeping his promises even when we don't keep ours. What is something God is doing in your life right now that demonstrates his love and compassion for you?

MAKING IT REAL: Decisions made after consulting and obeying God are never bad decisions. Pray that God will make his will known through his Word, his people, and his Spirit.

SMALL GROUP SESSION 12

✿

LESSON OBJECTIVE: To discover your strongholds and commit to trusting God to overcome them

Before the small group session read Chapter 12 of *Facing Your Giants*.

Scriptural Focus: 2 Samuel 5:1–12

THE CONTEXT: A lot of things happened between 2 Samuel 2 and 2 Samuel 5. You can go back and read the details if you like, but here's a brief summary. David was in Hebron but the location wasn't suitable as the center of a unified Israel. Through a series of conflicts, the nation was becoming more and more unified. Eventually, David reigns over all of Israel. Still he didn't have control of Jerusalem.

GETTING STARTED: Enlist a volunteer to read aloud 2 Samuel 5:1–12. Take a few minutes to establish the context for this passage.

DISCOVERING THE TRUTH: As you review this lesson in the study guide, use the following information and questions to help make the session applicable to the lives of the individuals in the class.

A BOLD MOVE: David defied the Jebusites and began to take control of Jerusalem. People said it couldn't be done, but they were wrong. David, with God's protection, made Jerusalem the capital of the unified nation. Describe a time when God overcame your doubts and accomplished something you might have believed to be impossible.

A Building Project: A stronghold usually has negative connotations, but David's stronghold represented protection from outside forces. How do you protect yourself and your family from the dangers in the world? Do you recognize the danger or do you believe yourself to be invincible?

An Impossible Result: As David penetrated Jerusalem he gained more control. He had children with concubines from Jerusalem and eventually did what the Jebusites said couldn't be done—he ruled Israel from within the walls of Jerusalem: the city of David! How is God making a difference through your life? What might he be accomplishing in and through the things you are involved in?

Making It Real: Strongholds can trap you. Pray that God will make you aware of the strongholds to which you are vulnerable and give you strength to overcome them.

SMALL GROUP SESSION 13

⚜

LESSON OBJECTIVE: To discover how we have made ordinary what God intends to be extraordinary and to commit to celebrating God's presence

Before the small group session read Chapter 13 of *Facing Your Giants*.

Scriptural Focus: 2 Samuel 6:1–19

THE CONTEXT: The ark of the covenant was a box that contained the Ten Commandments and represented God's presence with the Israelites. Before David's time, the ark had been captured by the Philistines but eventually sent away because of the bad things that accompanied their possessing it. It was in the care of Abinadab and his sons until David decided to take it to the temple in Jerusalem. There were strict rules associated with handling the ark—rules ignored by David and the people on the first attempt to move it. It was never to be carried on a cart, yet it was on a cart when the oxen stumbled, Uzzah reached for it, and died.

GETTING STARTED: Enlist a volunteer to read aloud 2 Samuel 6:1–19. Take a few minutes to establish the context for this passage.

DISCOVERING THE TRUTH: As you review this lesson in the study guide, use the following information and questions to help make the session applicable to the lives of the individuals in the class.

DIMINISHED RESPECT: If David knew about the rules for moving the ark, he ignored them. If he didn't know, he should have checked with someone before undertaking such a significant process with such carelessness. When it comes to God, err on the side of too much respect, not too little. If God's presence arrived in your church or home, how would you respond? Would you be bored, hope the service ended soon, be awed, or something else?

TRAGIC RESULTS: Disobedience to God has consequences. Period. The carelessness with which the ark was moved—including violating God's specific instructions regarding it—cost Uzzah his life and brought the party to an end. God's people should know better than to make a farce out of his presence. In what ways do people and churches suffer when they fail to give God the respect he demands? Why does God expect such respect from his people?

VICTORIOUS CELEBRATION: Finally David got it right and, three months later, he returned with priests and poles to move the ark in accordance with God's instructions. The ark's return to Jerusalem was cause for great celebration, which David led by dancing in the streets. In what areas of your life are you ignoring God's instructions? What do you think is God's response to your willing rebellion?

MAKING IT REAL: God is as distant as we make him. Through disobedience and rebellion, we put up a wall that separates us from God. Pray that God will help you understand how you should respond to his presence and make you aware of areas that you have placed off-limits to him.

SMALL GROUP SESSION 14

⌒⋀⌒

LESSON OBJECTIVE: To discover how God keeps his promises and to resolve to keep our promises to God and others

Before the small group session read Chapter 14 of *Facing Your Giants*.

Scriptural Focus: 2 Samuel 9:1–13

THE CONTEXT: Just before David began running from Saul, he had a conversation with Jonathan in which he promised to show kindness to Jonathan and his family. The promise had no statute of limitations; it was permanent. Of course, David had no idea what the implications of the promise would be. He simply made a promise he intended to keep. So, when life settled down, David had a chance to reflect on his eventful journey from the fields to the throne. He then remembered his promise to Jonathan. He could have easily side-stepped the responsibility, but he didn't. He intentionally looked for a way to fulfill the promise.

Mephibosheth was Jonathan's son. He was born healthy, but was injured when his nurse dropped him while escaping the battle that killed his father, Jonathan, and his grandfather, Saul. He was taken into the home of Machir in Lo Debar and was being cared for there.

GETTING STARTED: Enlist a volunteer to read aloud 2 Samuel 9:1–13. Take a few minutes to establish the context for this passage.

DISCOVERING THE TRUTH: As you review this lesson in the study guide, use the following information and questions to help make the session applicable to the lives of the individuals in the class.

A PROMISE REMEMBERED: There might have been no one other than David who knew about his promise to Jonathan. David was the king and, therefore, under no obligation to do anything he didn't want to do. But David's word mattered, so he inquired about the existence of a descendent of Jonathan. When you remember your promises, what do you do? Do you look for ways to fulfill them or look for ways to forget them? What promises have you made that are going unfulfilled?

A PROMISE IN ACTION: Remembering the promise was one thing; doing something about it was another. Sometimes we pacify ourselves by recounting our promises while ignoring opportunities to do what we said we'd do. David took action. He did more than glance around the room and say, "Nope, no one here from Jonathan's family!" He actually made an effort to locate someone who might know if Jonathan had any survivors. How much effort are you putting in to keeping the promises you have made to God, your spouse, your family, your employer, your friends, and your church? Is it easier to talk about your promises than to follow through on them? Why?

A PROMISE TO KEEP: David's integrity wouldn't allow him to ignore his promise to Jonathan. Your integrity (or lack of it) determines your responses to the promises you have made. We have an example in God—he keeps his promises to us even when we don't deserve them. When you accepted Jesus Christ as Lord, you were promised eternal life in heaven. Today you live with that promise reminding you that the bad things in life are only temporary.

You have some promises you expect others to keep, and there are some promises you are expected to keep. What are some things you can do to be more faithful in keeping your promises to God and other people?

MAKING IT REAL: God is faithful. We will never be as faithful as God, but we should never give up trying. Pray that God will help you remember your promises and give you the courage to act on the promises you have made and will make.

SMALL GROUP SESSION 15

✦

LESSON OBJECTIVE: To discover God's attitude toward arrogance and to commit to a life of humility

Before the small group session read Chapter 15 of *Facing Your Giants*.

Scriptural Focus: 2 Samuel 11:1–17

THE CONTEXT: David's kingdom was in good shape. They were free from external threats and focused their energies on expanding the territory and defeating minor opponents. In the spring, most kings accompanied their troops into battle. David, however, chose to stay home and sent Joab to lead the battle against Ammon and Rabbah. Because David wasn't where he should have been, he was exposed to temptation he should not have experienced. That's the way life goes! Maybe Bathsheba made a spectacle of herself. Maybe David went to great lengths to catch her bathing. It doesn't matter. The end result is the same—David committed adultery and tried to cover it up with murder. Known for his spiritual accomplishments, David now leaves a legacy of shame.

GETTING STARTED: Enlist a volunteer to read aloud 2 Samuel 11:1–17. Take a few minutes to establish the context for this passage.

DISCOVERING THE TRUTH: As you review this lesson in the study guide, use the following information and questions to help make the session applicable to the lives of the individuals in the class.

PURSUE HUMILITY: David's ego got the best of him. He was the king; times were good; he was popular. Where is the shepherd boy stooping by the brook to gather stones he would later use to slay Goliath? Where is the man asking God what he should do? People bent on doing what they want seldom stop to ask God for permission! What are some areas of your life where it is easy for your ego to take charge? What should you do when you begin thinking more of yourself than you should?

EMBRACE YOUR POVERTY: Everything David had was a result of God's goodness. God protected David from Goliath, Saul, the Philistines, his own men, and more. He made it possible for David to have Jerusalem when it appeared out of the question. Without God's riches, David was poor. You and I are the same! Everything we have is because of God's goodness. It's not because we are smart or talented or lucky. What are some things you take for granted that God has blessed you with? How should your knowledge of God's providence affect the way you approach each day?

RESIST THE PLACE OF CELEBRITY: David could have put on dark sunglasses and had his name up in lights . . . that's what some people live for. He did use his power as king to get what he wanted—Bathsheba. David already had wives, plenty of them! But rather than being satisfied with what he had, he desired what he didn't have. Does that sound familiar?

You can use your personal influence to get what you want, but what you want might not deliver what you expect. In what ways are you tempted to misuse your influence? What can you do to resist the temptation?

MAKING IT REAL: David never expected his encounter with Bathsheba to have such devastating consequences. He and Bathsheba were affected, but there was a lot of collateral damage. Pray that God will help you be aware of the dangers of disobedience and the consequences of stepping away from his guidance.

SMALL GROUP SESSION 16

⚜

LESSON OBJECTIVE: To understand God's omniscience and to commit to respecting his holiness and his Word

Before the small group session read Chapter 16 of *Facing Your Giants*.

Scriptural Focus: 2 Samuel 12:1–15

THE CONTEXT: David thought he had covered his tracks. Uriah was dead, Bathsheba was given the privilege of marrying the king, the illegitimate child would be legitimate, and they'd all live happily ever after . . . or would they? The one part of the story David neglected was God. God witnessed it all, knew about the cover-up, and dispatched a prophet named Nathan to confront David.

GETTING STARTED: Enlist a volunteer to read aloud 2 Samuel 12:1–15. Take a few minutes to establish the context for this passage.

DISCOVERING THE TRUTH: As you review this lesson in the study guide, use the following information and questions to help make the session applicable to the lives of the individuals in the class.

HOW CAN THAT BE? The parable told by Nathan illustrated the recklessness David used to take Bathsheba. David had no problem seeing the iniquity in the story; he simply refused to apply the same principles to his life. In what areas of life do you judge people more harshly than you judge yourself? In what areas of life is God's judgment situational?

WHO COULD THAT BE? David didn't get it. He was ready to have someone's head. He didn't see the story as a parallel to his actions. David pronounced a severe punishment—death! Then Nathan explained the story. The man who took the sheep when he had plenty was David. You can almost hear David gasp! What does God use to remind you of his laws and principles? Why is it so easy for us to apply them to others and excuse ourselves?

WHAT WILL IT COST? Sin has a penalty. David already had declared that death was the penalty for sheep-stealing. What should be the penalty for wife-stealing and murder? Undoubtedly David's humility resurfaced. He realized he wasn't above the law and that his actions would have long-term consequences. Why do we often not consider the long-term consequences of our actions?

MAKING IT REAL: David had been discovered. He was being held accountable for his actions. He received forgiveness but the tragic consequences already had been established. Forgiveness doesn't always circumvent consequences. Pray, asking God to forgive you of your sins and to make you aware of the consequences of disobeying him.

SMALL GROUP SESSION 17

∽✿∾

LESSON OBJECTIVE: To understand the value of one's family and to commit to giving your family the priority God expects

Before the small group session read Chapter 17 of *Facing Your Giants*.

Scriptural Focus: 2 Samuel 15:13–14; 30–31

THE CONTEXT: Trouble was brewing in the kingdom. David had been effective at everything except parenting. Parenting was near the bottom of his list of priorities. So far, so good. There were more than enough wives eight and countless concubines to care for the children he fathered, so why should he be concerned? But things got messy. Amnon, one of David's sons, took a liking to Tamar, one of David's daughters by a different mother. Amnon eventually raped Tamar and disposed of her like trash. Tamar told her brother, Absalom, and he revenged her rape by killing Amnon. Afraid that David would seek revenge on him, Absalom fled Jerusalem. But David did nothing to Absalom and did nothing for Tamar. He was silent. So, Absalom returned to Jerusalem and orchestrated a coup that forced David out of the city.

GETTING STARTED: Enlist a volunteer to read aloud 2 Samuel 15:13–14; 30–31. Take a few minutes to establish the context for this passage.

DISCOVERING THE TRUTH: As you review this lesson in the study guide, use the following information and questions to help make the session applicable to the lives of the individuals in the class.

RESPONSIBILITY IGNORED: David made everything except parenting important. His success in life is overshadowed by his failure at home. How can you make your responsibility at home more important? What things need to be eliminated from your life so you can make home a priority?

TROUBLE EXPERIENCED: When Amnon raped Tamar, David did nothing about it. In order to rule a nation he abdicated his throne at home. Years of neglect came back to haunt him. What does your home say about your leadership? Which is of more concern to you—your outside interests or your home? Explain your response.

A CHANGE NEEDED: Eight wives and numerous concubines produced for David more children than we can imagine. His personal conquest of the female population might have given his ego a boost, but it set in motion a sad series of events. By the time he was sixty, David's family was beyond repair. You, however, still have some time! In what ways do you need to change in order to make your family more important? How does your personal time with God affect your attitude toward your family and responsibilities at home?

MAKING IT REAL: You don't have to be like David. Pray asking God to help you make your family a priority and to help you say no to things that don't really matter.

SMALL GROUP SESSION 18

✥

LESSON OBJECTIVE: To discover how God enables his people to succeed in spite of their failure and commit to living in total dedication to God

Before the small group session read Chapter 18 of *Facing Your Giants*.

Scriptural Focus: 1 Chronicles 28:1–10

THE CONTEXT: For David, life was coming to an end. And what a life it had been! When we began, he was the unsuspecting heir to Saul's throne. We saw him kneeling by the brook collecting stones for the impending battle with Goliath and then running for his life as Saul's jealousy raged. He had moments of incredible victory and personal tragedy. He danced when the ark of the covenant arrived in Jerusalem and escaped when his son orchestrated a coup. Now he stands to address the people regarding his desire to build a temple—a permanent home for the ark.

GETTING STARTED: Enlist a volunteer to read aloud 1 Chronicles 28:1–10. Take a few minutes to establish the context for this passage.

DISCOVERING THE TRUTH: As you review this lesson in the study guide, use the following information and questions to help make the session applicable to the lives of the individuals in the class.

A LOFTY GOAL: Building a home for the ark of the covenant was certainly a worthy goal. It had been homeless since before the Philistines captured it. There was nothing wrong with what David wanted to do. Think about something you have wanted to do for God. What are the pros and cons of the work? Are there any reasons God might stop you from doing what you intend to do?

A GODLY ROADBLOCK: "But God" is a red light on David's path. He desired to build the temple, but God prevented him from doing so. Why? David said it was because he had been so violent. David had a way of disrespecting people in order to achieve his goals. What is it about you that might make God say "stop"? Is your attitude toward other people in line with God's attitude toward them? Is there any sin that you have yet to confess?

AN ACCURATE ASSESSMENT: David knew what his problem was but he didn't let that throw water on his fire. He knew from where he had come. He knew what God had done for him. He was aware of God's protection and provision. He had plenty to celebrate. What do you have to celebrate? How has God worked in your life to show you who he is and how much he loves you?

MAKING IT REAL: Rather than think about what you don't have or can't do, pray, thanking God for what he has done, is doing, and will do in and through your life.

SMALL GROUP SESSION 19

❧

LESSON OBJECTIVE: To remember how weak our giants are in light of God's strength and to commit to trusting God to strengthen us with his power

Before the small group session read Chapter 19 of *Facing Your Giants.*

Scriptural Focus: 1 Samuel 17:32–51

THE CONTEXT: We've been here before. David, the shepherd boy, was unwilling to let his God be trash-talked by Goliath. If no one else would stand up for God, David would . . . and he did. Saul tried to place his armor on David, but it was too heavy. David couldn't become something else; he was a shepherd with a cause. A staff (stick, if you will), five rocks, and a sling: those were not the weapons of champions. But little David knew something about giants. God is bigger and stronger!

GETTING STARTED: Enlist a volunteer to read aloud 1 Samuel 17:32–51. Take a few minutes to establish the context for this passage.

DISCOVERING THE TRUTH: As you review this lesson in the study guide, use the following information and questions to help make the session applicable to the lives of the individuals in the class.

THE STONE OF THE PAST: During his time with the sheep, David had seen God's power first hand. He had wrestled bears and lions in defense of his sheep and God stepped in and gave David victory. If God was so concerned about sheep, wouldn't he be more concerned about his people? What has God done in the past that gives you hope for the future?

THE STONE OF PRAYER: David knew that talking to God was the key to success. When he consulted God, things went well. When he left God out, life became chaotic. How can you make your prayer life more effective? When was the last time you sat and listened to God through prayer?

THE STONE OF PRIORITY: David saw Goliath as a chance for God to show off, not a chance for David to show off. If you make glorifying God a priority, you will discover his power to be even greater than you imagine. What are you doing to show God's greatness to those around you?

THE STONE OF PASSION: David was so passionate about his God that he pursued the giant. He didn't throw a stone and hide; he nailed Goliath between the eyes and then went to cut off his head. David wanted this giant gone for good. How can you rid yourself of your giants once and for all? What life changes do you need to make?

THE STONE OF PERSISTENCE: David had four more stones, and Goliath had four brothers. David wouldn't give up. One prayer might not be enough. Pray until you see things from God's perspective. After all, prayer isn't an effort for you to get God to see things your way! What do you need to pray about persistently? Make a prayer journal and keep track of your persistent prayers recording how God answers.

MAKING IT REAL: God has an abundant life available to anyone who will follow him. Pray, asking God to make his presence more real in your life everyday.

NOTES

NOTES

NOTES

NOTES

UPWORDS

Hope. Pure and simple.

The Teaching Ministry of Max Lucado

You're invited to partner with UpWords to bring radio and the Internet a message of hope, pure and simple, in Jesus Christ!

Visit www.maxlucado.com to find FREE valuable resources for spiritual growth and encouragement, such as:

- Archives of UpWords, Max's daily radio program. You will also find a listing of radio stations and broadcast times in your area.
- Daily devotionals
- Book excerpts
- Exclusive features and presentations
- Subscription information on how you can receive email messages from Max
- Downloads of audio, video, and printed material

You will also find an online store and special offers.

Call toll-free,
1-800-822-9673

for more information and to order by phone.

UpWords Ministries
P.O. Box 692170
San Antonio, TX 78269-2170
1-800-822-9673
www.maxlucado.com

Amazing Freedom 2007

Max Lucado first spoke at a Women of Faith conference in 2004 — and he's been back every year since! His stories of God's love and grace have touched us all. That's why we keep inviting him to be one of the few men among the tens of thousands of women at our events.

2007 is no exception: Max will join Women of Faith at several *Amazing Freedom* events. He'll help us become God focused and start knocking down our giants.

Don't miss Max and his message, *Facing Your Giants*, at the Women of Faith events listed below.

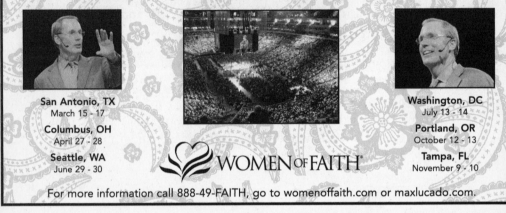

San Antonio, TX
March 15 - 17

Columbus, OH
April 27 - 28

Seattle, WA
June 29 - 30

WOMEN OF FAITH

Washington, DC
July 13 - 14

Portland, OR
October 12 - 13

Tampa, FL
November 9 - 10

For more information call 888-49-FAITH, go to womenoffaith.com or maxlucado.com.

Max Lucado Cards and Gifts from DaySpring

Touch someone's life and bring encouragement to their day with a Max Lucado greeting card or gift from DaySpring.

The Max Lucado line from DaySpring includes a large variety of products, including counter cards, a leather journal, coffee mugs, and more.

If you are looking for a way to share your heart and God's love in a powerful and meaningful way, look no further than DaySpring's selection of Max Lucado cards and gifts.

Find them today at a local Christian bookstore near you.

Share Your Heart and God's Love
www.dayspring.com

Other *Facing Your Giants* Products

Listen to the message of *Facing Your Giants* in your home or take it on the road. This CD makes the perfect gift for the family or friends you know are struggling to face their giants.

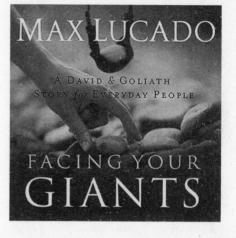

Facing Your Giants is also available in Spanish and Portuguese

BETANIA

You are not alone: 87 percent of workers don't find meaning in their work and 80 percent believe their talents are not used. And there are consequences—whether or not we realize it, our resulting attitude impacts our health, our relationships, our families and our fundamental sense of happiness. But best-selling author Max Lucado has a cure. We are all unique individuals, created in God's image, with our own gifts, strengths and passions. In his winsome, encouraging voice, Max will give readers practical tools for exploring and identifying our own uniqueness, motivation to put our uniqueness to work, and perspective to redefine our concept of work. It's never too late to uncover your strengths, discover God's will or redirect your career, and cure the otherwise hopeless prognosis of a common life.

Available in Spanish

Scientists assure us we can't live without water. But survival without God? We sip, we taste, but we often go without a drink from the Lord's well. And we pay the price. We shrink and hearts harden. This life-giving book leads us to the four nutrients needed by every soul. Come to the cross and know your sins are pardoned and your death is defeated. Receive Christ's energy and believe you can do all things through the One who gives you strength. Receive his Lordship, knowing you belong to Him and that He looks out for you. Receive His love and feel confident nothing can separate you from it.

For an audio/visual presentation and to learn more about *Come Thirsty*, visit www.maxlucado.com/come.thirsty

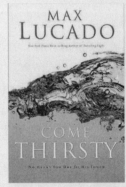

Available in Large Print and Spanish editions

Holiness in the filth of sheep manure and sweat. Divinity entering the world on the floor of a stable, through the womb of a teenager, and in the presence of a mere carpenter. God had come near! Travel back in time and relive Christ the Son of God becoming man.

In this stunning work, Max Lucado views the Savior who walked among us through a distinctly human lens. He speaks plainly to those of us who prefer to keep Jesus otherworldly, distant, and predictable: "Don't do it. For heaven's sake, don't. Let him into the mire and muck of our world. For only if we let him in can he pull us out."

Through vivid word pictures, come with Max as he brings to life the most important event in history . . . when *God Came Near*.

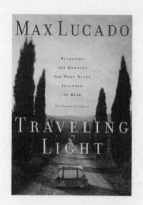

No wonder we get so weary—we're worn out from carrying excess spiritual baggage. Wouldn't it be nice to lose some of those bags? That's the invitation of Max Lucado. With the twenty-third Psalm as our guide, we learn to release some of the burdens we were never intended to bear. Learn to lighten your load, as Max embraces what it really means to say, "The Lord is my Shepherd."

Available in Large Print and Spanish editions

In this compelling quest for the Messiah, best-selling author Max Lucado invites readers to meet the blue-collar Jew whose claim altered a world and whose promise has never been equaled. Readers will come to know Jesus the Christ in a brand-new way as Lucado brings them full circle to the foot of the cross and the man who sacrificed his life on it.

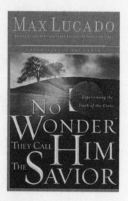

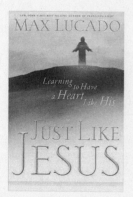

In his best-selling book *Just Like Jesus*, Max Lucado explains that God loves you just the way you are . . . but he refuses to leave you that way. Why? Because our ultimate goal should be a life that is just like Jesus. And with determination, faith, and God's help, we can all change for the better, no matter how long the bad habits have settled in.

THE CAMPAIGN TO MAKE
POVERTY HISTORY
WWW.ONE.ORG

There is a plague of biblical proportions taking place in Africa right now, but we can beat this crisis, if we each do our part. Step ONE is signing the ONE petition, to join the ONE Campaign.

The ONE Campaign is a new effort to rally Americans—ONE by ONE—to fight global AIDS and extreme poverty. We are engaging Americans everywhere we gather—in churches and synagogues, on the internet and college campuses, at community meetings and concerts. To learn more about The ONE Campaign, go to www.one.org and sign the online petition.

"Use your uniqueness to take great risks for God! If you're great with kids, volunteer at the orphanage. If you have a head for business, start a soup kitchen. If God bent you toward medicine, dedicate a day or a decade to AIDS patients. The only mistake is not to risk making one."

—Max Lucado, *Cure for the Common Life*

ONE Voice can make a difference.
Let God work through you; join the ONE Campaign now!

This campaign is brought to you by

Lucado Life Lessons Series

The Gospel of Mark
1-4185-0942-6

The Gospel of Luke
1-4185-0943-4

The Gospel of John
1-4185-0944-2

Acts
1-4185-0945-0

Romans
1-4185-0946-9

1 Corinthians
1-4185-0947-7

Revised and updated, the Lucado Life Lessons series is perfect
for small group or individual use and includes intriguing questions
that will take you deeper into God's Word.

NELSON IMPACT
A Division of Thomas Nelson Publishers
Since 1798

Available at your local Christian Bookstore